SCRIPTURE STUDY WORKBOOK:
THE BOOK OF MORMON

JARED HANSEN

Copyright © 2016 by Strait & Narrow Publishing

All rights reserved. Quoted passages are the property of their respective owners, as cited. No part of this book may be reproduced in any form without written consent from the publisher, Strait & Narrow Publishing 487 South 400 East Provo, UT 84606

This book is not affiliated with The Church of Jesus Christ of Latter-day Saints. All views and opinions are the author's alone and do not represent the Church.

ISBN — 978-1-53273-696-4

ALSO BY THE AUTHOR:

- Scripture Study Workbook: The Book of Mormon
- In Defense of Faith: Studying 8 Antichrists in The Book of Mormon
- Prayer, Pondering, & Paper Mountains: A Collection of Religious Essays

Visit the author's blog at thestraitandnarrow.tumblr.com for more inspiration and religious essays. Follow Strait & Narrow Publishing on Facebook to stay up to date on new books and other insider tips.

SCRIPTURE STUDY WORKBOOK:
THE BOOK OF MORMON

CONTENTS

Introduction 1

1 Nephi 3

2 Nephi 38

Jacob 89

Enos 100

Jarom 102

Omni 104

Words of Mormon 106

Mosiah 108

Alma 152

Helaman 242

3 Nephi 265

4 Nephi 307

Mormon 309

Ether 322

Moroni 344

Conclusion 360

Introduction

So you've decided to study the scriptures. This commandment to study daily is one that is difficult to start, and often unrewarding. This workbook is meant to assist you in your labors of studying the Book of Mormon. I've written questions for each chapter, designed to help you gain greater understanding of the doctrine.

This workbook is designed to be a companion for your studies, to assist you as you try to feast upon the word. I know that as we engage ourselves in the learning process, and seek to make scripture study an important part of our day, we will see miracles in our lives.

The Lord wants to pour out a multitude of blessings upon us as we incorporate the doctrine into our lives. Each chapter has five questions to prompt thought and an invitation to live what you've learned. There are also bonus questions to answer if you have the desire or the time.

You can answer as many questions as you want, or as few. This workbook is merely a guide to help you have the best scripture studies possible. If you are in need of additional inspiration, check out my book, "Feast Upon the Word," with seven tips on improving your scripture study.

1 Nephi 1

Basic:

1. Who is involved?
   Lehi, the people of Jerusalem, Nephi - family

2. What is being taught?
   Lehi trying to teach the people of Jerusalem
   Lehi teaching his family

3. Why is this important?
   Showing us the importance of obedience to the lord.

4. How do I apply what is taught?
   To strive to be ready for revelation at all times!

5. What can we learn about revelation from Lehi? Why are prophets called in each dispensation?
   He loved God, he obeyed. He tried to warn the people that he also loved.
   ~~A~~ Prophets are called to guide us.

Invitation:

Make time to share your testimony of revelation with someone. Or share your conversion story with a friend, coworker, or family member
→ Gave a talk in sacrement on revelation.

Bonus:

1. How does this chapter set the tone for the rest of the book? The rest of the Book of Mormon?
   It starts us off w/ Lehi's familys journey and their obedience to God.

2. Why do the Jews persecute Lehi? Where else is this pattern evident in the scriptures?

No one wants to be told they are wrong and sinning — All throughout the scriptures

3. Why will Jerusalem be destroyed? How is this relevant to us today?

Because they've all turned away from God. We need to learn to obey the prophet & God

* * * * *

1 Nephi 2

Basic:

1. Who is involved?

2. What is being taught?

3. Why is this important?

4. How do I apply what is taught?

5. What sacrifices has the Lord asked you to make in your life? Have you been willing to make them?

Invitation:

Write down how obedience has blessed your life. Reflect on an experience where you chose to be obedient and how the Lord blessed you for it.

Bonus:

1. What reservations do you have for consecrating all that you have to the building of the kingdom of God?

2. How can you relate to the exodus of Lehi's family into the wilderness? Have you had a similar experience leaving behind your comfort zone for something new and different?

3. Have you had a leadership role within or without the church? What can you learn from Nephi about presiding over others?

* * * * *

1 Nephi 3

Basic:

1. Who is involved?
   _____

2. What is being taught?
   _____
   _____

3. Why is this important?
   _____
   _____

4. How do I apply what is taught?
   _____
   _____

5. What can you learn about trials and afflictions from this chapter?
   _____
   _____
   _____
   _____

Invitation:

Share words of encouragement, either in person or in writing, with someone having a hard time.

Bonus:

1. What can we learn about Laban? Why is his story so vital?
   _____
   _____
   _____

2. Did you find Nephi's pep talk encouraging? Would you have returned for the plates if rejected once? Why or why not?

3. What sacrifices do you make for the scriptures? Are they an important part of your life?

4. How did Laman and Lemuel react to losing their property? How did Nephi react? How should we react in situations like this?

* * * * *

1 Nephi 4

Basic:

1. Who is involved?

2. What is being taught?

3. Why is this important?

4. How do I apply what is taught?

5. When has the Lord provided a way for you to accomplish his commandments?

Invitation:

Write about a tender mercy from the Lord in your life. It could be an experience where He has delivered someone or something into your hands.

Bonus:

1. Why was Nephi "led by the spirit"? How can we have similar experiences?

2. Why should we trust in the Lord? Despite our reservations, why should we be obedient?

3. What was the promise that Nephi made to Zoram? Who else makes similar promises to us?

_____
_____
_____
_____

* * * * *

1 Nephi 5

Basic:

1. Who is involved?
   Sariah + Lehi

2. What is being taught?
   Sariah learns that Lehi was really being led by God.

3. Why is this important?
   We need to trust others + God.

4. How do I apply what is taught?
   Try not to doubt + always follow God + prophets

5. What was the pattern for receiving revelation in this chapter? What can we learn about revelation and visions from Lehi's family?
   Lehi had a dream + shared w/ family ~
   We should be ready + prepared for revelation —

Invitation:

Write an entry in your journal about your experiences with family history.

Bonus:

1. How did Lehi react to his wives concerns? How should we react when our spouse is worried and distressed?

   He reasured her instead of getting mad.
   We should listen w/ respect and love —

2. Why did Lehi and Sariah offer sacrifices? How do we express our gratitude?

   Thats how they said thank you to God
   We should be saying Thankyou in our prayers

3. How did Lehi react to reading the plates? How can we search the scriptures like him?

   He was excited to learn his family history
   Read & study them.

* * * * *

1 Nephi 6

Basic:

1. Who is involved?

   Nephi

2. What is being taught?

    How to write in our journals like Nephi

3. Why is this important?

    to keep our personal Historys + testimonies

4. How do I apply what is taught?

    Try to write more in our journals

5. The missionary purpose is to "Invite others to come unto Christ by helping them receive the restored gospel." How is that similar to Nephi's purpose in keeping the records?

Invitation:

Invite someone to come unto Christ today. This could be sharing your testimony with a family member or friend. Or encouraging them to keep a commandment. Or having a spiritual experience with them.

Bonus:

1. Why was it important for Nephi to identify himself as a descendent of Joseph?

2. What are some things "pleasing unto God" that you can write about in your journal?

1 Nephi 7

Basic:

1. Who is involved?
   _____

2. What is being taught?
   _____
   _____

3. Why is this important?
   _____
   _____

4. How do I apply what is taught?
   _____
   _____

5. What did Nephi pray for? What did he receive from the Lord? Why were they different?
   _____
   _____
   _____
   _____

Invitation:

Ponder over a time where you prayed for something and the Lord answered it in a different way. What did you learn from that experience? Offer a prayer today that you will align your will to His.

Bonus:

1. Why was there a disagreement in the wilderness? Who wanted to return to Jerusalem and why?
   _____
   _____

_____
_____

2. Why did Nephi encourage his brethren to have faith? Why is faith always the answer?
_____
_____
_____
_____

3. What can we learn about forgiveness and repentance in this chapter?
_____
_____
_____
_____

*   *   *   *   *

1 Nephi 8

Basic:

1. Who is involved?
_____

2. What is being taught?
_____
_____

3. Why is this important?
_____
_____

4. How do I apply what is taught?
_____

5. What does the iron rod mean to you? What role has it played in your life? How about the strait and narrow?

Invitation:

Make a list of a few things you can do this week to stay on the strait and narrow.

Bonus:

1. Why would Lehi share his vision with his family?

2. Why does Nephi have a similar vision later in the book?

3. Why did Laman and Lemuel not partake of the fruit? How would you react to your son or daughter not partaking of the fruit?

4. What can you do to lead your family toward the tree of life?

_____
_____
_____

* * * * *

1 Nephi 9

Basic:

1. Who is involved?
   _____

2. What is being taught?
   _____
   _____

3. Why is this important?
   _____
   _____

4. How do I apply what is taught?
   _____
   _____

5. Have you ever followed a prompting without knowing why? How did that experience fortify your faith?
   _____
   _____
   _____
   _____

Invitation:

Memorize a scripture about faith.

Bonus:

1. What is the "special purpose" for Nephi keeping the records?

   _____
   _____
   _____
   _____

2. What does Nephi teach us about faith through his words and his actions? How can we have faith like Nephi?

   _____
   _____
   _____
   _____

*   *   *   *   *

1 Nephi 10

Basic:

1. Who is involved?

   _____

2. What is being taught?

   _____
   _____

3. Why is this important?

   _____
   _____

4. How do I apply what is taught?

   _____
   _____

5. What do we learn about the Holy Ghost in this chapter? What is its role in revelation?

   _____
   _____
   _____
   _____

Invitation:

   Meditate on the gift and power of the Holy Ghost. Search for its influence today through your actions.

Bonus:

1. Why were the Jews taken by the Babylonians? How is this a parable for mortality?

   _____
   _____
   _____
   _____

2. What are the differences between the three titles of the Lord in this chapter: Messiah, Savior, and Redeemer? What does this reveal about His role in our lives?

   _____
   _____
   _____
   _____

3. Why was it necessary for Christ to be baptized? Why are covenants and ordinances important to salvation?

   _____
   _____
   _____

4. Why do we learn about the scattering and gathering of the house of Israel? Why is this important?

*   *   *   *   *

1 Nephi 11

Basic:

1. Who is involved?

2. What is being taught?

3. Why is this important?

4. How do I apply what is taught?

5. Why does an angel appear to Nephi? How does this relate to revelation?

Invitation:

> Apply the pattern of Nephi by searching the scriptures, pondering their meaning, and praying to gain inspiration about something you're struggling with today.

Bonus:

1. Why does Nephi see Mary in this vision? What role does her story play in the Tree of Life parable?

2. Why does Nephi see the mortal ministry of the Savior? And why does Nephi mention these three events?

3. Why does Nephi describe the geography of his vision? Why was he "caught away to an exceedingly high mountain"?

* * * * *

1 Nephi 12

Basic:

1. Who is involved?

2. What is being taught?

3. Why is this important?

4. How do I apply what is taught?

5. What is the symbolism of calling the wicked "loathsome and filthy"? Why is this imagery used to describe the Lamanites?

Invitation:

Share your testimony of the Savior with a friend or family member today.

Bonus:

1. How does Nephi describe his seed who live in the land of promise?

2. What connections can you make between the children of Israel and the Nephites? Why are their histories similar? Why are they different?

3. Why would Christ appear to the children of Lehi in the Americas?

* * * * *

1 Nephi 13

Basic:

1. Who is involved?

2. What is being taught?

3. Why is this important?

4. How do I apply what is taught?

5. Can you list other prophets who have seen the Restoration or the building of Zion in the latter-days?

Invitation:

Write in your journal about the importance of the Restoration and how you are helping to build Zion.

Bonus:

1. Why does Nephi see the church of the devil in this vision? What role does it play in the parable of the Tree of Life?

2. What role does the apostasy play in the Plan of Salvation? Why is it crucial to our understanding of the Restoration?

3. What latter-day scripture came forth from the Restoration? How has it blessed your life and your testimony?

_____
_____

* * * * *

1 Nephi 14

Basic:

1. Who is involved?
   _____

2. What is being taught?
   _____
   _____

3. Why is this important?
   _____
   _____

4. How do I apply what is taught?
   _____
   _____

5. What does this chapter teach about persecution?
   _____
   _____
   _____
   _____

Invitation:

   Make a list of at least three things you are thankful for. Remember this list when things get tough, and you are persecuted for your beliefs.

Bonus:

1. What do we learn about the Gentiles in this chapter?

2. What makes the church of the devil "great and abominable"?

3. Why would the angel command Nephi to not write about everything he saw?

* * * * *

1 Nephi 15

Basic:

1. Who is involved?

2. What is being taught?

3. Why is this important?

   _____
   _____

4. How do I apply what is taught?

   _____
   _____

5. What does Nephi teach his brothers? What is the pattern for revelation and wisdom?

   _____
   _____
   _____
   _____

Invitation:

Make a plan for finding an answer to a concern you currently have. Outline the steps you'll take to receive revelation, exercise faith, and trust that you'll receive an answer.

Bonus:

1. Why is it important to learn about the scattering and gathering of Israel? How does this apply to us?

   _____
   _____
   _____
   _____

2. What can you learn about the vision of the Tree of Life from this chapter? How does Nephi's interpretation help you?

   _____
   _____
   _____
   _____

3. Why must God be just when dealing with the wicked? How can He meet the demands of justice, while still being merciful?

_____
_____
_____
_____

*   *   *   *   *

1 Nephi 16

Basic:

1. Who is involved?

_____

2. What is being taught?

_____
_____

3. Why is this important?

_____
_____

4. How do I apply what is taught?

_____
_____

5. Why do the wicked take the truth to be hard? Why is it so easy to become upset when asked to change?

_____
_____

_____
_____

Invitation:

    Watch the Mormon Message, "The Will of God." What can you learn from this parable of the gardener? Write your thoughts in your journal.

Bonus:

1. Why would messages appear and disappear on the sides of the Liahona? What application does this metaphor have in your life today?

_____
_____
_____
_____

2. What reactions do the children of Lehi have to Neohi breaking his bow? What should we do when we struggle with employment?

_____
_____
_____
_____

3. How can we avoid being chastened by an angel like Laman and Lemuel? What must we do to refrain from murmuring?

_____
_____
_____
_____

*   *   *   *   *

1 Nephi 17

Basic:

1. Who is involved?
   _____

2. What is being taught?
   _____
   _____

3. Why is this important?
   _____
   _____

4. How do I apply what is taught?
   _____
   _____
   _____
   _____

5. What ships have you been asked to build in your life? How have you reacted to these tasks presented by God?
   _____
   _____
   _____
   _____

Invitation:

Memorize a scripture about faith. Ponder over its meaning as you strive to be obedient to all the commands of the Lord.

Bonus:

1. Why would Nephi recount God's miracles with the children of Israel when exhorting his brethren to help build a ship? How does this apply to us today?

_____
_____
_____
_____

2. What power have you felt from the Spirit? How would you describe being filled with the Spirit?

_____
_____
_____
_____

3. Why should we follow Nephi's example in this chapter? What does he teach us about discipleship? Of faith in Christ? Of being a brother?

_____
_____
_____
_____

*   *   *   *   *

1 Nephi 18

Basic:

1. Who is involved?

_____

2. What is being taught?

_____
_____

3. Why is this important?

   _____
   _____

4. How do I apply what is taught?

   _____
   _____

5. What do we learn about obedience from Lehi's family in this chapter? Have you been asked to figuratively cross an ocean towards a promised land?

   _____
   _____
   _____
   _____

Invitation:

Share your testimony with a friend or family member about the blessings you've received from being obedient.

Bonus:

1. What do we learn about rebellion from Lehi's sons? Why weren't they successful in their endeavors?

   _____
   _____
   _____
   _____

2. How did Nephi react to being bound? How can we react to unjust persecution?

   _____
   _____
   _____
   _____

3. How can we endure the storms of life? Will we have a perfect life if we are righteous? Why or why not?

_____
_____
_____
_____

*   *   *   *   *

1 Nephi 19

Basic:

1. Who is involved?

    _____

2. What is being taught?

    _____
    _____

3. Why is this important?

    _____
    _____

4. How do I apply what is taught?

    _____
    _____
    _____

5. How often does Nephi mention being commanded of the Lord to keep a record on the plates? Why is it a priority to Nephi?

    _____
    _____

Invitation:

    Find and read from a journal of an ancestor.

Bonus:

1. Why would Nephi write about the plain and precious truths on the plates? Is it necessary for us to learn the deeper doctrine for salvation?

2. Why would Nephi write about the ministry and crucifixion of Christ? How does Nephi know of His coming?

3. What are some of the prophets that Nephi quotes in this chapter? Why are some not included in our canon today?

*   *   *   *   *

1 Nephi 20

Basic:

1. Who is involved?
   _____

2. What is being taught?
   _____
   _____

3. Why is this important?
   _____
   _____

4. How do I apply what is taught?
   _____
   _____

5. How has the Lord refined you? What is your furnace of affliction?
   _____
   _____
   _____
   _____

Invitation:

   Memorize a scripture about trials, hope, or adversity.

Bonus:

1. What makes the house of Israel the covenant people? Why does the Lord promise to protect them?
   _____
   _____
   _____

2. What water symbolism does the Lord use in this chapter? What do they represent? And how effective are they?

_____

*   *   *   *   *

1 Nephi 21

Basic:

1. Who is involved?

2. What is being taught?

3. Why is this important?

4. How do I apply what is taught?

5. What does it mean for Christ to say "I have graven thee upon the palms of my hands; thy walls are continually before me"? What is its importance to you?

_____
_____
_____

Invitation:

    Share your testimony of Christ to someone today.

Bonus:

1. Why does Nephi quote these Isaiah chapters? What is the message they convey?

   _____
   _____
   _____
   _____

2. Why is the symbolism in verse 15 meaningful? How does it apply to you?

   _____
   _____
   _____
   _____

3. How does Christ free the prisoners? What does this represent? How have you been redeemed by Christ?

   _____
   _____
   _____
   _____

*   *   *   *   *

1 Nephi 22

Basic:

1. Who is involved?
   _____

2. What is being taught?
   _____
   _____

3. Why is this important?
   _____
   _____

4. How do I apply what is taught?
   _____
   _____

5. What does this chapter teach about the final days? Why does this chapter bring hope to us in the latter-days?
   _____
   _____
   _____
   _____

Invitation:

   Provide an act of service today to encourage someone to smile.

Bonus:

1. Why must God punish the wicked? Why are they burned as stubble?
   _____
   _____
   _____

2. Why won't the kingdom of the devil succeed? How is Satan gaining power today?

___

3. Verse 3 mentions that Nephi has mentioned temporal and spiritual things. How does the Lord use both to teach eternal truths? How are temporal and spiritual lessons connected?

___

*   *   *   *   *

2 Nephi 1

Basic:

1. Who is involved?
   _____

2. What is being taught?
   _____
   _____

3. Why is this important?
   _____
   _____

4. How do I apply what is taught?
   _____
   _____

5. What does Lehi teach about the mercies of God? Can you relate a tender mercy from your life?
   _____
   _____
   _____
   _____

Invitation:

What plans have you made to put on the armor of God daily? Do your best today to fulfill this goal.

Bonus:

1. What do we learn about the role of a father from Lehi? How can we emulate his strengths in our parenting?
   _____
   _____

2. What does Lehi teach about the purpose of life? At the end of his life what does he do?

3. What does Lehi encourage Laman and Lemuel to do? How can we follow his counsel to "arise from the dust"?

*   *   *   *   *

2 Nephi 2

Basic:

1. Who is involved?

2. What is being taught?

3. Why is this important?

4. How do I apply what is taught?

5. What does Lehi teach about the need for a Redeemer? How does this role differ from Christ's other titles?

Invitation:

Lighten someone's' load today, and redeem them from their troubles.

Bonus:

1. How do the events of the Atonement and the Fall of Adam and Eve relate? Can one exist without the other? Why or why not?

2. What do we learn about agency? Why was the War in Heaven fought over our ability to choose?

3. What are the consequences for choosing the right? What rewards have you seen as you choose liberty and eternal life?

2 Nephi 3

Basic:

1. Who is involved?
   _____

2. What is being taught?
   _____
   _____

3. Why is this important?
   _____
   _____

4. How do I apply what is taught?
   _____
   _____

5. What Josephs are mentioned in this chapter? How are they related to each other? Why would Nephi include these prophecies?
   _____
   _____
   _____
   _____

Invitation:

Talk to a family member or friend about Joseph Smith, and discuss his role in history.

Bonus:

1. Why would the prophets of the past prophesy about the Restoration? Why did it matter to them? Should it matter to us?
   _____
   _____
   _____

2. The scrap of the coat of many colors is taught to be symbolic of what? What else could it represent?

   _____
   _____
   _____
   _____

3. Why does God call seers in each dispensation? Does God have favorite prophets? Should we?

   _____
   _____
   _____
   _____

*   *   *   *   *

2 Nephi 4

Basic:

1. Who is involved?
   _____

2. What is being taught?
   _____
   _____

3. Why is this important?
   _____
   _____

4. How do I apply what is taught?

5. What are the blessings Lehi leaves on his different children?

Invitation:

Review your patriarchal blessing, or take steps towards obtaining one.

Bonus:

1. This chapter is often referred to as "the Psalm of Nephi." Why? What connections does it share with the book of Psalms?

2. Why would Nephi write about the goodness of God? How do you think he was feeling after the death of his father?

3. What do we learn about faith from Nephi? How are trust and faith connected? Trust and hope?

2 Nephi 5

Basic:

1. Who is involved?
   _____

2. What is being taught?
   _____
   _____

3. Why is this important?
   _____
   _____

4. How do I apply what is taught?
   _____
   _____
   _____

5. Why was it important for Nephi to build a temple? Do you value temple attendance?
   _____
   _____
   _____
   _____

Invitation:

Make a goal to visit the temple as soon as possible. Browse pictures of temples online and meditate on their importance.

Bonus:

1. Why would the Lamanites separate themselves from the Nephites? What do we learn from this sad story?
   _____
   _____

2. How were Nephi and his descendants able to keep the Law of Moses? What resource did they rely on for the gospel?

3. Why would Nephi teach his people to be industrious? What does Nephi teach about the value of hard work? How does this apply to his "go and do" mentality?

*   *   *   *   *

2 Nephi 6

Basic:

1. Who is involved?

2. What is being taught?

3. Why is this important?

4. How do I apply what is taught?

5. What does verse 6 mean? How will the Gentiles assist the children of Israel?

Invitation:

Make a family mission plan, outlining how you will participate in missionary work this year. Or if you have one, achieve one of your goals today.

Bonus:

1. Why would Nephi allow his younger brother a chance to write in the plates? What opportunities can we give our siblings and family members to build their faith?

2. What does Jacob testify about? How can you focus on the mission and ministry of Christ?

3. Why would Jacob recount Jewish history? What are some temporal lessons we learn from the history of the Israelites? Spiritual lessons?

2 Nephi 7

Basic:

1. Who is involved?

2. What is being taught?

3. Why is this important?

4. How do I apply what is taught?

5. What does Isaiah teach about the Messiah? Why would this be important to Jacob?

Invitation:

Memorize a scripture about Jesus Christ.

Bonus:

1. How can we give our backs to the smiters? How should respond to criticism and adversity?

2. How can we find strength in Christ? Why is it crucial to learn about His ministry and role?

3. What can we learn from verses 10 & 11? Why is the metaphor of fire and sparks used?

*   *   *   *   *

2 Nephi 8

Basic:

1. Who is involved?

2. What is being taught?

3. Why is this important?

4. How do I apply what is taught?

5. What are some ways that the Lord is comforting Zion? Gathering Israel?

Invitation:

Outline a plan for how you can build Zion. Come up with actionable steps that will strengthen your faith, the testimonies of your family, and magnify your calling.

Bonus:

1. What might "the dragon" represent? Why this metaphor?

2. What does the imagery suggest in this chapter? Why would Isaiah mention the desert, desolation, and destruction?

3. What does verse 24 mean to you? How do you put on your beautiful garments?

_____

_____

_____

_____

* * * * *

2 Nephi 9

Basic:

1. Who is involved?

_____

2. What is being taught?

_____

_____

3. Why is this important?

_____

_____

4. How do I apply what is taught?

_____

_____

5. How are the Atonement and the Fall related? Why must we rely on our Savior?

_____

_____

_____

_____

Invitation:

> Draw out the Plan of Salvation. Place it in a prominent place where you will see it regularly.

Bonus:

1. What does Jacob teach about the spirit world? What inspired you in this chapter?

   _____
   _____
   _____
   _____

2. Describe truths about the Plan of Salvation learned from this chapter.

   _____
   _____
   _____
   _____

3. Why is Christ the keeper of the gate? What does this role mean to you?

   _____
   _____
   _____
   _____

* * * * *

2 Nephi 10

Basic:

1. Who is involved?

   _____

2. What is being taught?

   _____
   _____

3. Why is this important?

   _____
   _____

4. How do I apply what is taught?

   _____
   _____

5. When will the Jews be restored? Why is this important to know?

   _____
   _____
   _____
   _____

Invitation:

   Memorize a scripture about mercy or grace.

Bonus:

1. What can we learn about the Jews from this chapter? How are these lessons applicable to us?

   _____
   _____
   _____
   _____

2. How is salvation tied to grace? What role does mercy play in attaining the Celestial Kingdom?

   _____
   _____
   _____

3. Should mercy be on our "checklist"? Why do we focus on performing the ordinances of salvation instead of receiving the grace of Christ?

*   *   *   *   *

2 Nephi 11

Basic:

1. Who is involved?

2. What is being taught?

3. Why is this important?

4. How do I apply what is taught?

5. Who else delighted in the scriptures? How can we find scripture study to be a joy and delight?

_____
_____

Invitation:

    Bring joy into someone's life today. Perform a simple act of service, such as an honest compliment, to bring a smile to someone else's face.

Bonus:

1. What five things does Jacob mention as a delight unto him? How are these things related?

   _____
   _____
   _____
   _____

2. When have you delighted in sharing your testimony of Christ? What can you do to increase your missionary efforts?

   _____
   _____
   _____
   _____

3. What are your treasures? What brings you delight?

   _____
   _____
   _____
   _____

*   *   *   *   *

2 Nephi 12

Basic:

1. Who is involved?
   _____

2. What is being taught?
   _____
   _____

3. Why is this important?
   _____
   _____

4. How do I apply what is taught?
   _____
   _____

5. Why would Isaiah delight in the Salt Lake Temple? What does it represent?
   _____
   _____
   _____
   _____

Invitation:

Share your testimony of temple work with someone today.

Bonus:

1. Why does Isaiah prophesy about the millennium? How do you feel about the Second Coming?
   _____
   _____
   _____

2. Why are the proud and the wicked punished during the final judgment? Why is this warning given?

* * * * *

2 Nephi 13

Basic:

1. Who is involved?

2. What is being taught?

3. Why is this important?

4. How do I apply what is taught?

5. Why is it important to know that Christ is our mediator and our judge? Why would he plead our case, and decide our reward?

_____
_____
_____

Invitation:

    Forgive someone today.

Bonus:

1. Why must the prophets remind us that disobedience brings punishment? Why does Satan lie and say wickedness is happiness?

   _____
   _____
   _____
   _____

2. What does verse 15 mean to you? What does it mean symbolically to "beat [the] people to pieces, and grind the faces of the poor"?

   _____
   _____
   _____
   _____

3. The chapter ends with imagery of the daughters of Zion. What does this imagery mean to you? Why are the daughters of Zion punished in this way?

   _____
   _____
   _____
   _____

*   *   *   *   *

2 Nephi 14

Basic:

1. Who is involved?
   _____

2. What is being taught?
   _____
   _____

3. Why is this important?
   _____
   _____

4. How do I apply what is taught?
   _____
   _____

5. Why dies Nephi teach about the redemption of Zion? Which meaning of Zion do you think he is describing? (The children of Israel, the Kingdom of God, the Church of Christ, the physical city...)
   _____
   _____
   _____
   _____

Invitation:

Explain what Zion means to you in your journal today.

Bonus:

1. What dose verse 1 mean to you? How is this prophecy being fulfilled today?
   _____
   _____
   _____

2. Verse 6 describes place of refuge. What places in your life offer spiritual safety? What actions provide spiritual protection?

* * * * *

2 Nephi 15

Basic:

1. Who is involved?

2. What is being taught?

3. Why is this important?

4. How do I apply what is taught?

5. Why are we constantly taught about the scattering and gathering of Israel? Why is this a source of comfort for the sons of Lehi?

_____
_____
_____

Invitation:

    Visit FamilySearch.org and check out your family tree. Learn the names of your ancestors.

Bonus:

1. In what ways have you been symbolically "scattered"? How has the Lord gathered you like a hen gathering her chicks?
_____
_____
_____
_____

2. Why is humility necessary to gaining exaltation? Why does the pride cycle include actions that compel people to be humble?
_____
_____
_____
_____

3. Why is the symbol of an ensign used in this chapter? What does the word ensign mean?
_____
_____
_____
_____

*   *   *   *   *

2 Nephi 16

Basic:

1. Who is involved?

2. What is being taught?

3. Why is this important?

4. How do I apply what is taught?

5. How can we compare Isaiah's experience to sacrament meeting? What similarities are there between this chapter, and what occurs each Sabbath?

Invitation:

Write your thoughts and feelings at your next sacrament meeting.

Bonus:

1. Why were Isaiah's sins forgiven before he was called to serve?

2. What role did the seraphim play in this chapter?

3. What does the coal represent? How else is fire mentioned in the scriptures?

*   *   *   *   *

2 Nephi 17

Basic:

1. Who is involved?

2. What is being taught?

3. Why is this important?

4. How do I apply what is taught?

5. What does verse 15 mean to you?

Invitation:

Invite or encourage someone to be obedient today.

Bonus:

1. What is significant of the virgin birth of Christ? Why was this an integral part of ancient prophecies about His coming?

2. What food items are mentioned in this chapter? What might they represent?

* * * * *

2 Nephi 18

Basic:

1. Who is involved?

2. What is being taught?

   _____
   _____

3. Why is this important?

   _____
   _____

4. How do I apply what is taught?

   _____
   _____

5. Why would the Lord be compared to a stumbling stone? What does that mean to you?

   _____
   _____
   _____
   _____

Invitation:

   View the paintings of Christ in your home, chapel, or browse online. If you have space, find a place to hang a new painting.

Bonus:

1. What rocks of offense have you encountered in your life? How have you overcome them?

   _____
   _____
   _____
   _____

2. Where should we turn for guidance? Why?

   _____
   _____
   _____

3. Why are "peeping wizards" mentioned in this chapter? How do they contribute to the overall message?

_____

* * * * *

2 Nephi 19

Basic:

1. Who is involved?

_____

2. What is being taught?

_____

3. Why is this important?

_____

4. How do I apply what is taught?

_____

5. What titles of Christ are mentioned in this chapter? Why would Isaiah include all of them?

_____

_____
_____

Invitation:

    Memorize a scripture about the Atonement.

Bonus:

1. How does this chapter support your testimony of the Savior?

_____
_____
_____
_____

2. What is the symbolism of verse 2? How is Christ the light that shineth in darkness?

_____
_____
_____
_____

3. What parables also relate to the principle taught in verse 18? Why are the wicked burned as stubble during the final judgment?

_____
_____
_____
_____

*　　*　　*　　*　　*

2 Nephi 20

Basic:

1. Who is involved?

2. What is being taught?

3. Why is this important?

4. How do I apply what is taught?

5. Why would the destruction of Assyria represent the destruction of the wicked? What does the nation of Assyria symbolize to the people of Israel?

Invitation:

Map out the pride cycle, and include specifics of each step.

Bonus:

1. Why would Nephi quote this chapter from Isaiah? How is this important to the children of Israel and the seed of Lehi?

2. How does verse 15 relate to missionary work? As disciples of Christ, should we be proud of the work we do? Why or why not?

_____

* * * * *

2 Nephi 21

Basic:

1. Who is involved?

2. What is being taught?

3. Why is this important?

4. How do I apply what is taught?

5. Who was the son of Jesse? Why would it be important for Christ to be the stem of Jesse?

_____
_____
_____

Invitation:

    Pray and then look for an opportunity to share the gospel today.

Bonus:

1. Why must the knowledge of God cover the earth in the Millennium? What does this mean for missionary work now?

   _____
   _____
   _____
   _____

2. Why the imagery of wolves, calves, lions, and children? What do these verses mean to you?

   _____
   _____
   _____
   _____

3. How is the Lord gathering Israel now? What ensigns are being raised by the Lord?

   _____
   _____
   _____
   _____

                *   *   *   *   *

2 Nephi 22

Basic:

1. Who is involved?

2. What is being taught?

3. Why is this important?

4. How do I apply what is taught?

5. How can we turn away the anger of the Lord? How will our Savior comfort us?

Invitation:

Comfort someone in need of support today. Listen to their concerns, and offer to help in any way you can.

Bonus:

1. What does verse 2 mean to you? How do trust, hope, faith, and love relate to each other?

2. Why should we sing hymns? What does verse 5 teach about the spiritual nature of music?

* * * * *

2 Nephi 23

Basic:

1. Who is involved?

2. What is being taught?

3. Why is this important?

4. How do I apply what is taught?

5. Why does Isaiah teach about the destruction of Babylon? Why would this matter to us?

_____
_____

Invitation:

    Sing "Israel, Israel, God is Calling," (Hymn #7), and meditate on its meaning.

Bonus:

1. How does this chapter relate to chapter 20? Compare and contrast.

_____
_____
_____
_____

2. Why the celestial imagery in verse 10? How could this relate to the title of Christ, The Light of the World?

_____
_____
_____
_____

3. How can we receive the mercy of Christ? Why are the children of Israel repeatedly warned about the consequences of sin?

_____
_____
_____
_____

*   *   *   *   *

2 Nephi 24

Basic:

1. Who is involved?

2. What is being taught?

3. Why is this important?

4. How do I apply what is taught?

5. Why was Lucifer cast out? How can we avoid similar punishment?

Invitation:

Memorize a scripture about obedience.

Bonus:

1. Why would the Israelites be promised millennial rest?

2. What feelings does this chapter stir within you? How does this chapter relate to the Plan of Salvation?

___

* * * * *

2 Nephi 25

Basic:

1. Who is involved?

2. What is being taught?

3. Why is this important?

4. How do I apply what is taught?

5. How does this chapter relate to Nephi's mission as a prophet scribe?

Invitation:

    Read a few passages from your journal. Reflect on the power of record-keeping.

Bonus:

1. What does Nephi promise in verse 4? How can we understand the words of Isaiah?

   _____
   _____
   _____
   _____

2. What key points of the ministry of the Savior does Nephi prophesy? Why do they matter to Nephi, and why do they matter to you?

   _____
   _____
   _____
   _____

3. Why does Nephi mention the story about the children of Israel in verse 20?

   _____
   _____
   _____
   _____

*   *   *   *   *

2 Nephi 26

Basic:

1. Who is involved?

   _____

2. What is being taught?

3. Why is this important?

4. How do I apply what is taught?

5. Why does it matter that Christ ministered to the Nephites?

Invitation:

Discuss the role of our Savior with a family member or friend today.

Bonus:

1. How is the prophecy fulfilled that the Nephites will cry from the dust?

2. Why are priestcrafts, secret combinations, and false churches condemned by the Lord?

3. Why are we nothing without charity? Why are we nothing without the love of Christ?

* * * * *

2 Nephi 27

Basic:

1. Who is involved?

2. What is being taught?

3. Why is this important?

4. How do I apply what is taught?

5. Why was the coming forth of the Book of Mormon prophesied? Why would Nephi find it important?

Invitation:

> Discuss your testimony of the Book of Mormon with someone today.

Bonus:

1. How is apostasy a form of darkness? Why are these two mentioned in this chapter?

   _____
   _____
   _____
   _____

2. Why do "learned men" reject the Book of Mormon? Why is it important to accept this book of scripture?

   _____
   _____
   _____
   _____

3. Why is the Restoration called "a marvelous work and a wonder"?

   _____
   _____
   _____
   _____

* * * * *

2 Nephi 28

Basic:

1. Who is involved?

   _____

2. What is being taught?

   _____
   _____

3. Why is this important?

   _____
   _____

4. How do I apply what is taught?

   _____
   _____

5. Why is it important to know about the establishment of false churches?

   _____
   _____
   _____
   _____

Invitation:

> Reflect on what makes a good gospel teacher. Make a list of attributes or qualities they exemplify.

Bonus:

1. What are some foolish doctrines taught today? Why are many deceived by these false churches?

   _____
   _____
   _____
   _____

2. How can we protect ourselves from false teachers and apostasy?

   _____
   _____
   _____

3. Why is the devil so bent on our destruction? How does he produce rage in the hearts of men?

_____

_____

_____

_____

* * * * *

2 Nephi 29

Basic:

1. Who is involved?

2. What is being taught?

3. Why is this important?

4. How do I apply what is taught?

5. What is the real reason that the Gentiles say "We don't need another Bible"?

_____
_____

Invitation:

    Write a list of things you enjoy about the Bible.

Bonus:

1. Why does Heavenly Father allow His children to accept or reject the Book of Mormon?

_____
_____
_____
_____

2. Why does the Lord speak to many nations? How does this prove His divinity or His role as Savior and Redeemer?

_____
_____
_____
_____

3. Why will the world be judged out of the books which will be written?

_____
_____
_____
_____

*　*　*　*　*

2 Nephi 30

Basic:

1. Who is involved?

2. What is being taught?

3. Why is this important?

4. How do I apply what is taught?

5. Why is the doctrine of "covenant people" so important to Nephi and Isaiah? Why should it be important to us?

Invitation:

Sing "I am a Child of God," (Hymn #301), and meditate on its meaning.

Bonus:

1. Why is it important to make covenants? What are the blessings associated with keeping our covenants?

2. How is Israel being restored? What must happen before the Second Coming?

3. We are taught repeatedly that when we are righteous we are blessed, and when we are wicked we are punished. Is obedience really that simple? Why or why not?

* * * * *

2 Nephi 31

Basic:

1. Who is involved?

2. What is being taught?

3. Why is this important?

4. How do I apply what is taught?

5. Why was Christ baptized, and why should we follow His example?

Invitation:

Share your testimony of baptism with someone today.

Bonus:

1. Why are repentance and baptism the gate to the strait and narrow path?

2. How do we receive eternal life? Why does the Lord use the metaphor of a path or road?

3. Why is the gospel of Jesus Christ composed of these five elements: faith, repentance, baptism, receiving the gift of the Holy Ghost, and enduring to the end? Why only these five principles and ordinances?

2 Nephi 32

Basic:

1. Who is involved?
   _____

2. What is being taught?
   _____
   _____

3. Why is this important?
   _____
   _____

4. How do I apply what is taught?
   _____
   _____

5. Why do angels speak by the power of the Holy Ghost? And how is this communication the words of Christ?
   _____
   _____
   _____
   _____

Invitation:

Pray for and act upon inspiration from the Holy Ghost today.

Bonus:

1. How else can we feast upon the words of Christ? Where do we find them (besides the scriptures)?
   _____
   _____
   _____

2. What does Nephi teach about gaining understanding? What does he prescribe if we can't understand the scriptures?

3. What should we do if we are filled with doubts? Where can we turn for truth?

* * * * *

2 Nephi 33

Basic:

1. Who is involved?

2. What is being taught?

3. Why is this important?

4. How do I apply what is taught?

5. What does this chapter teach us about the power of the Book of Mormon? Why is it impossible to believe the words of Christ and not cherish the Book of Mormon?

Invitation:

Write in your journal your testimony of the Book of Mormon.

Bonus:

1. In verses 1-3, Nephi describes the process he went through in writing upon the plates. What does he teach us about leadership? How can we teach our children and family the doctrines of the Kingdom?

2. What does Nephi teach us about bearing our testimonies? How can we emulate his example when sharing the gospel?

3. What does verse 12 teach about prayer?

*   *   *   *   *

Jacob 1

Basic:

1. Who is involved?
   _____

2. What is being taught?
   _____
   _____

3. Why is this important?
   _____
   _____

4. How do I apply what is taught?
   _____
   _____

5. What does Jacob teach about discipleship in verse 7?
   _____
   _____
   _____
   _____

Invitation:

Memorize a scripture about repentance.

Bonus:

1. How have you been blessed by keeping the commandments? What strength does your testimony give you?
   _____
   _____
   _____

2. What sin were the people guilty of in verse 15? Why is this a problem today?

___

3. What is the root of all evil? How does this contribute to the pride cycle?

___

*   *   *   *   *

Jacob 2

Basic:

1. Who is involved?

___

2. What is being taught?

___

3. Why is this important?

___

4. How do I apply what is taught?

___

5. What does Jacob teach about the law of Chasity in this chapter?

Invitation:

Write the doctrine of and blessings associated with the law of Chastity.

Bonus:

1. How does Jacob preface this chapter and the chastisement it contains? How can we call our family, friends, and loved ones to repentance like Jacob?

2. Why is the law of Chastity so important? Why then does Satan belittle its significance today as in the past?

3. What does Jacob teach about marriage in this chapter? How are we responsible for our spouse and our children?

4. Why would the Lord delight in the chastity of women? How are we held accountable for our actions against the daughters of God?

_____
_____
_____
_____

Jacob 3

Basic:

1. Who is involved?

_____

2. What is being taught?

_____
_____

3. Why is this important?

_____
_____

4. How do I apply what is taught?

_____
_____

5. Why do the pure in heart receive the word of God as "pleasing"? Why do the wicked have a different reaction?

_____
_____
_____
_____

Invitation:

Share your testimony of repentance with a family member or friend.

Bonus:

1. How can we become pure in heart? What holds us back from this virtue?

   _____
   _____
   _____
   _____

2. Why are the Lamanites less wicked than the Nephites? What does this mean to us?

   _____
   _____
   _____
   _____

3. Why are we warned against fornication and lasciviousness?

   _____
   _____
   _____
   _____

*   *   *   *   *

Jacob 4

Basic:

1. Who is involved?

   _____

2. What is being taught?

   _____
   _____

3. Why is this important?

   _____
   _____

4. How do I apply what is taught?

   _____
   _____

5. Why have all prophets taught and worshiped Christ? What does this mean to you?

   _____
   _____
   _____
   _____

Invitation:

Reflect upon your testimony of Christ while watching a Bible Video on LDS.org.

Bonus:

1. How is Christ the center of your worship? How can you seal His teachings into your heart?

   _____
   _____
   _____
   _____

2. Can you think of other acts or stories in the scriptures that are in similitude of Christ?

   _____
   _____
   _____
   _____

3. What does this chapter teach about the Atonement?

   _____
   _____

4. What is the foundation stone spoken of in this chapter? Why will the Jews reject it?

*   *   *   *   *

Jacob 5

Basic:

1. Who is involved?

2. What is being taught?

3. Why is this important?

4. How do I apply what is taught?

5. What does this chapter teach about the history of the earth? Where does this allegory fit into the Plan of Salvation?

_____
_____

Invitation:

> If you can, visit a garden or farm and eat fresh produce. Ponder on the work and effort involved in growing fruit trees.

Bonus:

1. Why is it important to know about the scattering and gathering of Israel? Why such a focus on this doctrine in the first books of the Book of Mormon?

   _____
   _____
   _____
   _____

2. Why does the Lord teach us about the Jews and the Gentiles? What can this represent to us today?

   _____
   _____
   _____
   _____

*   *   *   *   *

Jacob 6

Basic:

1. Who is involved?

   _____

2. What is being taught?

   _____

3. Why is this important?

4. How do I apply what is taught?

5. Why will the Lord recover Israel in the latter-days? What binds Him to fulfill this promise?

Invitation:

Memorize a scripture about Israel.

Bonus:

1. How do we avoid the lake of fire and brimstone? What steps and choices do we make daily to stay on the path to salvation?

2. Do you think the burning of the world is literal or figurative? How so?

3. Why would this sermon be important to the people of Jacob's day? They were just falling into iniquity and breaking the law of Chastity.

___
___
___
___

* * * * *

Jacob 7

Basic:

1. Who is involved?

   ___

2. What is being taught?

   ___
   ___

3. Why is this important?

   ___
   ___

4. How do I apply what is taught?

   ___
   ___

5. What do we learn about the role of antichrists from this chapter? Will there be those who antagonize our faith?

   ___
   ___
   ___

Invitation:

> Make a list of everything you enjoy about the gospel of Jesus Christ. Compare that to a list of everything you enjoy about the church of Christ.

Bonus:

1. What are the tenants of Sherem's teachings? Why are these contrary to the laws of God?

2. What does Jacob teach about Christ? Why would this counter the words of Sherem?

3. Why would Mormon include this account in his abridging of the plates?

*   *   *   *   *

Enos

Basic:

1. Who is involved?
   _____

2. What is being taught?
   _____
   _____

3. Why is this important?
   _____
   _____

4. How do I apply what is taught?
   _____
   _____

5. Why does Enos offer this prayer? What was his reasoning behind it?
   _____
   _____
   _____
   _____

Invitation:

Wrestle with God in prayer today.

Bonus:

1. In the previous chapter, Jacob mentions that he will pass the responsibility of recordkeeping to his son Enos. When have you felt inadequate following your call to serve?
   _____
   _____
   _____

_____

2. Why did Enos use the phrasing "my soul hungered"?

_____
_____
_____
_____

*   *   *   *   *

Jarom

Basic:

1. Who is involved?
   _____

2. What is being taught?
   _____
   _____

3. Why is this important?
   _____
   _____

4. How do I apply what is taught?
   _____
   _____

5. What does Jarom teach about the history of his people? How have the Lamanites and the Nephites prospered?
   _____
   _____
   _____
   _____

Invitation:

Memorize a scripture about obedience.

Bonus:

1. Why does Jarom mention those who were "stiffnecked" in verse 4? What does this word mean to you?
   _____
   _____

2. What does verse 11 teach about the roles of prophets? What is the role of the Church and its leaders in relation to our faith?

* * * * *

Omni

Basic:

1. Who is involved?
   _____

2. What is being taught?
   _____
   _____

3. Why is this important?
   _____
   _____

4. How do I apply what is taught?
   _____
   _____

5. What does this chapter teach about the history of civilizations? What comparisons and contrasts can you find between the Nephites, the Mulekites, and the Jaredites?
   _____
   _____
   _____
   _____

Invitation:

Visit your bookshelf and find books that have changed your life. Make an effort to read these books more often.

Bonus:

1. Why would the Lord preserve the records of the Jaredites? Why would He preserve the Mulekites for the Nephites to find?
   _____
   _____

_____
_____

2. What do we learn about record keeping from Amaron and Chemish? When did Amaron write upon the plates?

_____
_____
_____
_____

*   *   *   *   *

Words of Mormon

Basic:

1. Who is involved?
   _____

2. What is being taught?
   _____
   _____

3. Why is this important?
   _____
   _____

4. How do I apply what is taught?
   _____
   _____

5. Why was this chapter included in the Book of Mormon?
   _____
   _____
   _____
   _____

Invitation:

Sing as many verses of "Follow the Prophet," (Children's Songbook #110) as you can. Reflect on the impact of ancient prophets.

Bonus:

1. Why was Mormon called to be a prophet historian? How did his calling as compiler of the plates assist his calling as a prophet?
   _____
   _____
   _____

2. What did Mormon have to say about the Small Plates of Nephi? What truths have you found in these initial 6 books?

* * * * *

Mosiah 1

Basic:

1. Who is involved?
   _____

2. What is being taught?
   _____
   _____

3. Why is this important?
   _____
   _____

4. How do I apply what is taught?
   _____
   _____

5. Why did King Benjamin value his sons' education? What did he teach them?
   _____
   _____
   _____
   _____

Invitation:

Share your testimony of the importance of education with a family member or friend.

Bonus:

1. What role do the scriptures play in civilization? What role do they play in your life?
   _____
   _____
   _____
   _____

2. Why will the Lord preserve these records? Why did He bring about the Book of Mormon?

___
___
___
___

3. Why does this chapter end with a description of the Liahona? What does it teach us about magnifying our calling?

___
___
___
___

* * * * *

Mosiah 2

Basic:

1. Who is involved?

___

2. What is being taught?

___
___

3. Why is this important?

___
___

4. How do I apply what is taught?

5. What lessons do you learn about King Benjamin? What did he do as a leader that you can emulate?

Invitation:

Write in your journal what you believe makes a good leader.

Bonus:

1. Why was King Benjamin's address so important? What events in our lives are of similar magnitude?

2. Why is it important to serve? What do you learn about service from this sermon?

3. Why is rebellion a sin? How does it relate to faith? Humility?

Mosiah 3

Basic:

1. Who is involved?
   _____

2. What is being taught?
   _____
   _____

3. Why is this important?
   _____
   _____

4. How do I apply what is taught?
   _____
   _____

5. Why does King Benjamin teach about the ministry of Christ? How does this relate to his sermon on service?
   _____
   _____
   _____
   _____

Invitation:

Memorize a scripture about Jesus Christ.

Bonus:

1. What does this chapter teach about the Atonement?
   _____
   _____
   _____

2. What is the difference between the natural man and a saint? How do we become saints and gain exaltation?

   _____
   _____
   _____

3. What role does the Atonement play in our religion? What is the center of our faith?

   _____
   _____
   _____
   _____

*   *   *   *   *

Mosiah 4

Basic:

1. Who is involved?

   _____

2. What is being taught?

   _____
   _____

3. Why is this important?

   _____
   _____

4. How do I apply what is taught?

   _____

5. What does this chapter teach about forgiveness?

Invitation:

Research the doctrine of forgiveness.

Bonus:

1. How are repentance and forgiveness different? How are they similar?

2. Why would King Benjamin teach about consecration and repentance in the same chapter?

3. How can we serve those who are less fortunate than us?

*   *   *   *   *

Mosiah 5

Basic:

1. Who is involved?

2. What is being taught?

3. Why is this important?

4. How do I apply what is taught?

5. How do we become the sons and daughters of Christ? With this in mind, how is Christ the Father and the Son?

Invitation:

Post an inspirational note about being a child of God.

Bonus:

1. Why are we called by the name of Christ? How does this chapter relate to our baptismal covenants? The words of the sacramental prayers?

2. What does verse 12 mean to you? Why must His name be written on our hearts?

3. Why must we be steadfast and immovable? How do we exemplify these characteristics in our lives?

* * * * *

Mosiah 6

Basic:

1. Who is involved?

2. What is being taught?

3. Why is this important?

4. How do I apply what is taught?

5. How does the Lord call men and women as leaders in the church?

Invitation:

    Make a list of attributes of a great Relief Society president. Compare to the attributes of a great Primary president, or a great Elder's Quorum president, or a great Sunday School president.

Bonus:

1. Why does the Lord call priests and teachers to consult with the people?

2. What does verse 7 teach about the reign of King Mosiah? What did he do as king, and what were the results?

*   *   *   *   *

Mosiah 7

Basic:

1. Who is involved?

2. What is being taught?

3. Why is this important?

4. How do I apply what is taught?

5. Why did Ammon leave Zarahemla? What did he find?

Invitation:

Express gratitude at least five times today.

Bonus:

1. Why was Limhi so glad to meet Ammon? What do we learn about the history of the people?

2. What was the counsel of King Limhi to his people in verse 19? How does this counsel apply to us today?

_____
_____
_____
_____

3. What were the weaknesses of Zeniff? How can we avoid being deceived by cunning and crafty men like the Lamanite king?

_____
_____
_____
_____

*   *   *   *   *

Mosiah 8

Basic:

1. Who is involved?
_____

2. What is being taught?
_____
_____

3. Why is this important?
_____
_____

4. How do I apply what is taught?
_____

5. What do we learn about prophets, seers, and revelators in this chapter?

Invitation:

Bear your testimony about following the prophet to a friend or family member today.

Bonus:

1. How does this chapter relate to the translation of the Book of Mormon?

2. Why are the holy records so important to the Nephite prophets? Do any other works of scripture contain such an emphasis on the compilation of sacred writings? Why or why not?

3. What does this chapter teach about spiritual gifts? Are there any gifts that are not spiritual in nature?

Mosiah 9

Basic:

1. Who is involved?
   _____

2. What is being taught?
   _____
   _____

3. Why is this important?
   _____
   _____

4. How do I apply what is taught?
   _____
   _____

5. What does Zeniff warn about in verse 3? Why is this mentioned by Mormon?
   _____
   _____
   _____
   _____

Invitation:

Offer two or three more prayers today than usual.

Bonus:

1. What were the sins of the Lamanite people described in this chapter? What adjectives were used to describe them?
   _____
   _____
   _____
   _____

2. Why were the people of Zeniff at war with the Lamanites? Were they successful?

3. How can we cry mightily to the Lord for deliverance? Why would this be important?

*   *   *   *   *

Mosiah 10

Basic:

1. Who is involved?

2. What is being taught?

3. Why is this important?

4. How do I apply what is taught?

5. What does this chapter teach about relying on the Lord?

___

Invitation:

Ask someone how they have relied on the Lord.

Bonus:

1. What can we learn about emergency preparedness from this chapter?

___

2. Why do we have accounts like this about the battles between the Nephites and the Lamanites? What can these wars represent?

___

3. What does verse 12 teach about the power of offense? What can we do to prevent becoming a "wild, and ferocious, and a blood-thirsty people"?

___

* * * * *

Mosiah 11

Basic:

1. Who is involved?
   _____

2. What is being taught?
   _____
   _____

3. Why is this important?
   _____
   _____

4. How do I apply what is taught?
   _____
   _____

5. What are the sins of King Noah? Why was he a terrible king?
   _____
   _____
   _____
   _____

Invitation:

Be generous with your time, talents, or resources today.

Bonus:

1. Why are the wicked priests consumed with riotous living? Why is this a sin?
   _____
   _____
   _____
   _____

2. Why do the people hate Abinadi? Why are the prophets unpopular?
   _____
   _____
   _____
   _____

3. What does this chapter teach about the law of Chastity?
   _____
   _____
   _____
   _____

*   *   *   *   *

Mosiah 12

Basic:

1. Who is involved?
   _____

2. What is being taught?
   _____
   _____

3. Why is this important?
   _____
   _____

4. How do I apply what is taught?
   _____
   _____

5. What was unfair about Abinadi's trial?

Invitation:

Memorize a scripture about persecution.

Bonus:

1. How should we react when our beliefs are mocked? How can we emulate Abinadi?

2. Why will many misinterpret the scriptures? How could the wicked priests quote scriptures in their defense?

3. Why are the Ten Commandments central to Abinadi's teaching?

* * * * *

Mosiah 13

Basic:

1. Who is involved?

2. What is being taught?

3. Why is this important?

4. How do I apply what is taught?

5. Why or why not will the Lord protect us in times of trouble? How can we receive this blessing?

Invitation:

Ask someone about the blessings they've received for being obedient.

Bonus:

1. What does this chapter teach about salvation? Why must we turn to the Savior for exaltation?

2. Why is it incredible that God will pay for our sins? Why is the divinity of Christ important to His mission?

3. What do we learn about the relationship between knowledge and belief? Why does salvation not come from understanding the law of Moses?

*   *   *   *   *

Mosiah 14

Basic:

1. Who is involved?

2. What is being taught?

3. Why is this important?

4. How do I apply what is taught?

   _____
   _____

5. Why would Abinadi quote Isaiah while on trial? How can we rely on the words of the prophets in our times of persecution?

   _____
   _____
   _____
   _____

Invitation:

Reflect on a time when you found peace and comfort in the words of the prophets.

Bonus:

1. Did Christ only suffer for our sins? Why is it meaningful for Him to feel all our pains and anguish?

   _____
   _____
   _____
   _____

2. Why was Christ humiliated and persecuted? Why is this important for His intercession on our behalf?

   _____
   _____
   _____
   _____

3. What do verses 4 and 5 mean to you? What does the symbolism mean to you?

   _____
   _____
   _____
   _____

Mosiah 15

Basic:

1. Who is involved?

2. What is being taught?

3. Why is this important?

4. How do I apply what is taught?

5. How is Christ both the Father and the Son? Why does this matter to our testimony?

Invitation:

Share your testimony of the Atonement.

Bonus:

1. What does it mean that Christ will make an intercession for us? How is this wording similar and different to "atone" "mediation" and "redeem"?

2. What do we learn about the role of prophets in this chapter? Why should we accept their teachings?

3. Why is the Resurrection meaningful? Why is it a part of the Plan of Salvation?

* * * * *

Mosiah 16

Basic:

1. Who is involved?

2. What is being taught?

3. Why is this important?

4. How do I apply what is taught?

5. How are the Fall and the Atonement connected? Why do we need to be redeemed?

Invitation:

Sing hymn #185 "Reverently and Meekly Now." Reflect on its message.

Bonus:

1. Why do the wicked remain in their carnal state? Why is the natural man a part of our nature?

2. What does verse 9 mean to you? Why does Christ symbolize light?

3. How did the law of Moses teach about the ministry of Christ?

Mosiah 17

Basic:

1. Who is involved?
   _____

2. What is being taught?
   _____
   _____

3. Why is this important?
   _____
   _____

4. How do I apply what is taught?
   _____
   _____

5. What do we learn from Alma? Why is it important to heed the teachings of our prophets and leaders?
   _____
   _____
   _____
   _____

Invitation:

Compliment your best friend today. Express gratitude for their friendship.

Bonus:

1. Why did Noah almost release Abinadi? What changed his mind?
   _____
   _____
   _____

2. Are the wicked free from consequences? Why or why not?

* * * * *

Mosiah 18

Basic:

1. Who is involved?

2. What is being taught?

3. Why is this important?

4. How do I apply what is taught?

5. Why does Alma teach and baptize the people? Why is baptism important?

_____
_____

Invitation:

    Memorize a scripture about baptism.

Bonus:

1. What do we learn about conversion from this chapter? Will it be easy to follow Christ? Why or why not?

   _____
   _____
   _____
   _____

2. Why was it important for the newly called priests and teachers to teach nothing but repentance and faith?

   _____
   _____
   _____
   _____

3. When will we be forced to flee into the wilderness like the people of Alma?

   _____
   _____
   _____
   _____

*   *   *   *   *

Mosiah 19

Basic:

1. Who is involved?
   _____

2. What is being taught?
   _____
   _____

3. Why is this important?
   _____
   _____

4. How do I apply what is taught?
   _____
   _____

5. Why did King Noah lose favor in the eyes of the Gideon and the people?
   _____
   _____
   _____

Invitation:

Perform an act of compassion today.

Bonus:

1. Why did the Lamanites invade the land? Why will some affliction come because of our wickedness?
   _____
   _____
   _____

2. What do we learn about leadership from this chapter? Why is it important to love the people you serve?

3. How can we show compassion to those we don't like?

* * * * *

Mosiah 20

Basic:

1. Who is involved?

2. What is being taught?

3. Why is this important?

4. How do I apply what is taught?

   _____
   _____

5. Why is it important to understand the facts before we jump to conclusions? Do we always know the thoughts and intents of others?

   _____
   _____
   _____
   _____

Invitation:

   Make an effort to listen more than you speak today.

Bonus:

1. Why did the priests of Noah abduct the daughters of the Lamanites? Why was this a foolish and selfish act?

   _____
   _____
   _____
   _____

2. What do we learn about the importance of communication in this chapter? How can this chapter be a metaphor for our relationships with others?

   _____
   _____
   _____
   _____

3. What do we learn about the importance of oaths and promises to the children of Lehi? How could we benefit from a similar attitude?

   _____
   _____
   _____
   _____

Mosiah 21

Basic:

1. Who is involved?
   _____

2. What is being taught?
   _____
   _____

3. Why is this important?
   _____
   _____

4. How do I apply what is taught?
   _____
   _____

5. Why were the people of Limhi persecuted? What does verse 4 mean?
   _____
   _____
   _____
   _____

Invitation:

Share your testimony of how a trial was a blessing in disguise.

Bonus:

1. Why do you think the people of Limhi were converted to Ammon's teachings? How do our trials humble us?
   _____
   _____
   _____

2. What do we learn about the importance of priesthood authority from this chapter? Why couldn't the people be baptized?

3. Why would it be important to the people of Limhi to share the Jaredite plates with Ammon?

* * * * *

Mosiah 22

Basic:

1. Who is involved?

2. What is being taught?

3. Why is this important?

4. How do I apply what is taught?

5. Who came up with the plan of escape? Why is it important to listen to everyone regardless of title or authority?

Invitation:

Counsel with someone about a problem you're facing, and consider their advice.

Bonus:

1. What do we learn about bondage and trials from this chapter? How did the people exercise faith?

2. What do the Lamanite guards teach us? How can we avoid a similar fate?

*   *   *   *   *

Mosiah 23

Basic:

1. Who is involved?

2. What is being taught?

3. Why is this important?

4. How do I apply what is taught?

5. Why does Alma refuse to be king? Is this related to their experience with Noah?

Invitation:

Memorize a scripture about humility.

Bonus:

1. Why is it more important to be a spiritual leader within our homes than a temporal leader? How can we emphasize spiritual learning as parents?

2. What does this chapter teach about chastisement? What can you learn from your current trial or difficulty?

3. How are Amulon and Alma different in regards to leadership? Who would you prefer to be your leader and why?

* * * * *

Mosiah 24

Basic:

1. Who is involved?

2. What is being taught?

3. Why is this important?

4. How do I apply what is taught?

5. How is this different than the exodus of the people of Limhi in chapter 22?

Invitation:

Pray for someone in need today, multiple times if necessary.

Bonus:

1. Why should we continue to pray always?

2. Why would the Lord make their burdens appear to be light? Will we always be delivered from our trials and afflictions?

3. When did the people of Alma express thanks for their deliverance? When should we show gratitude?

Mosiah 25

Basic:

1. Who is involved?
   _____

2. What is being taught?
   _____
   _____

3. Why is this important?
   _____
   _____

4. How do I apply what is taught?
   _____
   _____

5. How does this chapter relate to the doctrine of the scattering and gathering of the House of Israel? What groups of people were lost and then reunited through the gospel?
   _____
   _____
   _____
   _____

Invitation:

Reach out to someone who is lost or in need of rescue.

Bonus:

1. What can we hypothesize about Mosiah and Alma's relationship? How did they work together?
   _____
   _____

2. Why would the Nephites gather in their capital city of Zarahemla? What does this teach about the building of Zion?

* * * * *

Mosiah 26

Basic:

1. Who is involved?

2. What is being taught?

3. Why is this important?

4. How do I apply what is taught?

5. What does this chapter teach about forgiveness and repentance?

Invitation:

    Memorize a scripture about repentance.

Bonus:

1. Why would the unbelievers lead away members of the Church? How does this example relate to Lehi's vision?

2. Why was Alma promised eternal life? How can we obtain this promise?

3. What does this chapter teach about missionary work? What can we do to improve our missionary efforts?

*   *   *   *   *

Mosiah 27

Basic:

1. Who is involved?

2. What is being taught?

3. Why is this important?

4. How do I apply what is taught?

5. What responsibility do we have as members of the church to ensure religious equality? Why can't we persecute others?

Invitation:

Research a belief system you know little about.

Bonus:

1. What do verses 4 and 5 teach about self-reliance? Why is this an eternal principle?

2. What do we learn about the actions of our youth? Is it impossible to prevent our children from making poor choices? Why or why not?

_____
_____
_____
_____

3. How can we have a change of heart like Alma the younger (besides seeing angels)? Why is it important to be born of the Spirit?

_____
_____
_____
_____

*   *   *   *   *

Mosiah 28

Basic:

1. Who is involved?

_____

2. What is being taught?

_____
_____

3. Why is this important?

_____
_____

4. How do I apply what is taught?

_____

5. Why do the sons of Mosiah desire to preach to the Lamanites? What does this teach us about those who are ready to accept the gospel?

Invitation:

Find a missionary opportunity today such as bearing testimony, sharing a Mormon Message, or encouraging a visit to Mormon.org.

Bonus:

1. In verse 5 we read that the sons of Mosiah pleaded for many days to preach to the Lamanites. Why would Mosiah be hesitant to let his sons serve among the Lamanites? What do we learn from Mosiah about letting our children serve missions?

2. What two groups approached King Mosiah in this chapter? What were their requests? How did Mosiah react to each?

3. Why is translation a spiritual gift? How does it relate to us?

Mosiah 29

Basic:

1. Who is involved?
   _____

2. What is being taught?
   _____
   _____

3. Why is this important?
   _____
   _____

4. How do I apply what is taught?
   _____
   _____

5. Why would Mosiah propose the reign of judges instead of kings? What happened in the previous chapter to influence this decision?
   _____
   _____
   _____
   _____

Invitation:

Write in your journal about an experience where scripture study changed your life for the better.

Bonus:

1. What do we learn in this chapter about leadership? Why is it better for us to fill the role of judge than king in our families?
   _____
   _____
   _____

2. Why did the people love Mosiah? How can we leave a legacy for our posterity?

_____
_____
_____
_____

* * * * *

Alma 1

Basic:

1. Who is involved?

2. What is being taught?

3. Why is this important?

4. How do I apply what is taught?

5. Why do priestcrafts and persecutions spread among the people? Why are these common to all generations?

Invitation:

Memorize a scripture about service.

Bonus:

1. What crime was Nehor punished for and why?

2. What drove Nehor to commit his sins? What do you think were his motivations?

3. What does verse 26 teach about laboring in the church? Why is it important for us to minister like Christ?

* * * * *

Alma 2

Basic:

1. Who is involved?

2. What is being taught?

3. Why is this important?

4. How do I apply what is taught?

5. What does Amlici teach about offense?

Invitation:

Bury a weapon of rebellion; give up a "favorite sin" or vice.

Bonus:

1. Is it wise to rebel against the church of God? Why or why not?

2. Who will be the ultimate victor in the last days? Why are we taught that good will triumph over evil repeatedly?

3. Why do you think Alma, the spiritual and governmental leader, led the armies against Amlici?

Alma 3

Basic:

1. Who is involved?

2. What is being taught?

3. Why is this important?

4. How do I apply what is taught?

5. Why are the Amlicites cursed? Is this a symbolic cursing, or literal?

Invitation:

Forgive someone who has wronged you. Find a way to let go of a grudge.

Bonus:

1. Why would the Lord discourage the covenant people from intermarrying the heathen peoples? Why was this stressed with the Israelites?

2. What can we learn about temple marriage and covenants from this chapter?

_____
_____
_____
_____

3. What are some consequences of sin?

_____
_____
_____
_____

*   *   *   *   *

Alma 4

Basic:

1. Who is involved?

_____

2. What is being taught?

_____
_____

3. Why is this important?

_____
_____

4. How do I apply what is taught?

_____

5. What does verse 10 mean? Why would the wickedness of church members be a stumbling block to those outside the faith?

Invitation:

Sing hymn #130 "Be Thou Humble." Reflect on its message.

Bonus:

1. What do we learn about conversion and baptism from this chapter? Why would Mormon include this miracle of thousands being baptized?

2. Why is social inequality a trial to the church? Why is it a part of the pride cycle?

3. What does this chapter teach about service? About ministering to others? Or charity?

* * * * *

Alma 5

Basic:

1. Who is involved?
   _____

2. What is being taught?
   _____
   _____

3. Why is this important?
   _____
   _____

4. How do I apply what is taught?
   _____
   _____

5. What are the steps to salvation outlined in this chapter?
   _____
   _____
   _____
   _____

Invitation:

Memorize a scripture about repentance or humility.

Bonus:

1. Why is humility necessary to cleanse us from sin?
   _____
   _____
   _____
   _____

2. How do pride and envy hold us back from repenting and keeping the commandments?

   _____
   _____
   _____
   _____

3. What does verse 47 mean to you? How did Alma gain his testimony of these things?

   _____
   _____
   _____
   _____

* * * * *

Alma 6

Basic:

1. Who is involved?

   _____

2. What is being taught?

   _____
   _____

3. Why is this important?

   _____
   _____

4. How do I apply what is taught?

   _____
   _____

5. Why is the word of God liberal for all? And how does it liberate us?

Invitation:

Share your testimony of missionary work.

Bonus:

1. What was the church commanded to do? How did they invite others into the fold?

2. What do we learn about missionary work from this chapter?

* * * * *

Alma 7

Basic:

1. Who is involved?

2. What is being taught?

3. Why is this important?

4. How do I apply what is taught?

5. What does this chapter teach about the Atonement?

Invitation:

Set a goal, and write a plan to develop a Christ-like attribute.

Bonus:

1. How does Christ loose the bands that bind us? How does his ministry release us from bondage?

2. Why the symbolism of filthiness? How does this relate to repentance?

3. How are humility, faith, hope, and charity related?

Alma 8

Basic:

1. Who is involved?

2. What is being taught?

3. Why is this important?

4. How do I apply what is taught?

5. Why did Alma leave Ammonihah? Why did he return?

Invitation:

Memorize a scripture about missionary work.

Bonus:

1. What does this chapter teach about member missionary work? How can we be like Amulek for the full-time missionaries?

2. Why should we follow the promptings of the Spirit? What do we learn about revelation from Alma and Amulek?

3. Why was Amulek an asset for Alma in the city of Ammonihah? Why did Amulek preach with Alma?

* * * * *

Alma 9

Basic:

1. Who is involved?

2. What is being taught?

   _____
   _____

3. Why is this important?

   _____
   _____

4. How do I apply what is taught?

   _____
   _____

5. Why is repentance such a common theme in these chapters? Why would Mormon preserve these accounts?

   _____
   _____
   _____
   _____

Invitation:

   Sing hymn #115 "Come, Ye Disconsolate." Reflect on its invitation to repent.

Bonus:

1. Why will the Lord be merciful to the Lamanites? How is this a warning for us today?

   _____
   _____
   _____
   _____

2. What is taught about Jesus Christ?

   _____
   _____
   _____
   _____

3. Why are the Nephites protected as long as they're righteous? Have you seen an example of this in your life?

_____
_____
_____
_____

*   *   *   *   *

Alma 10

Basic:

1. Who is involved?
_____

2. What is being taught?
_____
_____

3. Why is this important?
_____
_____

4. How do I apply what is taught?
_____
_____

5. What do we learn about our righteous desires and prayers in this chapter?
_____
_____
_____
_____

Invitation:

> Pray earnestly for a righteous desire, more than usual.

Bonus:

1. Why would it matter if Lehi descended from Manasseh? What promises are tied to the tribe of Manasseh?

   _____
   _____
   _____
   _____

2. Why do the wicked lawyers and judges preclude the destruction of the people?

   _____
   _____
   _____
   _____

*   *   *   *   *

Alma 11

Basic:

1. Who is involved?

   _____

2. What is being taught?

   _____
   _____

3. Why is this important?

   _____

4. How do I apply what is taught?

5. Why would Mormon include the Nephite monetary system in this chapter? How does it relate to the narrative?

Invitation:

Make time for the things that matter most, instead of pursuing riches.

Bonus:

1. Why is it important to know that Christ will not save us in our sins, but from our sins?

2. Why will all men rise in immortality? Why is this a comforting doctrine?

3. What does this chapter teach about the repentance and the Resurrection? How are they related?

* * * * *

Alma 12

Basic:

1. Who is involved?

2. What is being taught?

3. Why is this important?

4. How do I apply what is taught?

5. How do we learn the "mysteries of god"? Why is there effort required on our part?

Invitation:

Share your testimony about the benefits of scripture study and revelation.

Bonus:

1. What are we judged upon? How are thoughts, beliefs, words, and works related?

2. Alma preaches about the plan of redemption. Why is it also called the plan of happiness and the plan of salvation?

3. What does it mean to have a remission of our sins?

* * * * *

Alma 13

Basic:

1. Who is involved?

2. What is being taught?

3. Why is this important?

4. How do I apply what is taught?

5. What is the primary role of all callings in the church?

Invitation:

Memorize a scripture about service.

Bonus:

1. What does this chapter teach about the priesthood?

2. What does verse 12 mean to you?

* * * * *

Alma 14

Basic:

1. Who is involved?

2. What is being taught?

3. Why is this important?

4. How do I apply what is taught?

5. Did the wicked people of Ammonihah thwart the kingdom of God? Why were their actions in vain?

Invitation:

Sing hymn #129 "Where Can I Turn for Peace." Reflect on its message.

Bonus:

1. Why are Alma and Amulek imprisoned? Will the work of God always be accepted? Why or why not?

2. Why do bad things happen to innocent people? What does this chapter teach about justice?

3. What does this chapter teach about trials? How will the Lord redeem us?

* * * * *

Alma 15

Basic:

1. Who is involved?

2. What is being taught?

3. Why is this important?

4. How do I apply what is taught?

5. What does Zeezrom teach us? How must we be converted like him?

Invitation:

Ask someone about how they have been healed through the power of God.

Bonus:

1. What do we learn about feeling godly sorrow, and its relation to repentance?

2. What are the key doctrines of priesthood blessings? What have you learned from your experience receiving and/or giving priesthood blessings?

*   *   *   *   *

Alma 16

Basic:

1. Who is involved?

2. What is being taught?

3. Why is this important?

4. How do I apply what is taught?

5. What does verse 5 teach about humility? Why should we look for advice from spiritual leaders?

Invitation:

Share your testimony of humility.

Bonus:

1. Why were the people of Ammonihah destroyed? Was the Lord just in fulfilling His promise?

2. Why would the Nephites desire to drive the Lamanites out of their land? What could this symbolize in our lives?

3. What do we learn about inequality from Alma and Amulek? Why is the gospel free for all who believe?

*   *   *   *   *

Alma 17

Basic:

1. Who is involved?

2. What is being taught?

3. Why is this important?

4. How do I apply what is taught?

5. What did the sons of Mosiah do to have the spirit of prophecy? Why would this be important as missionaries?

Invitation:

Make an effort to fast and pray more earnestly than usual.

Bonus:

1. Why did the sons of Mosiah split up in the land of the Lamanites?

2. Why did Ammon seek to be the King's servant? Why did he reject the offer to marry one of Lamoni's daughters?

3. What can we learn from Ammon about missionary work? How can we emulate his example?

Alma 18

Basic:

1. Who is involved?

2. What is being taught?

3. Why is this important?

4. How do I apply what is taught?

5. How does Ammon teach King Lamoni? Why would he employ this teaching style?

Invitation:

Acquire a copy of "Teaching: No Greater Call," and make a plan to implement its principles.

Bonus:

1. Why is King Lamoni terrified of Ammon? How can our fears bring us closer to God?

2. Why would it be important for Ammon to teach about Christ?

3. How did Lamoni react to Ammon's teaching? How can we emulate his desire?

* * * * *

Alma 19

Basic:

1. Who is involved?

2. What is being taught?

3. Why is this important?

4. How do I apply what is taught?

5. What do we learn about Ammon from verse 6?

Invitation:

Share your testimony of the Savior with a family member or friend.

Bonus:

1. What does the queen teach us about faith? Why did Ammon praise her for her faith?

2. Why did Ammon pray in verse 14? What are good motivations for us to pray?

3. What does Abish teach us about missionary work? About wanting to find those who need the truth?

* * * * *

Alma 20

Basic:

1. Who is involved?
   _____

2. What is being taught?
   _____
   _____

3. Why is this important?
   _____
   _____

4. How do I apply what is taught?
   _____
   _____

5. Why was Lamoni desirous for his father to meet with the missionaries? How was he filled with the spirit of Elijah?
   _____
   _____
   _____
   _____

Invitation:

Memorize a scripture about missionary work.

Bonus:

1. How can we deliver our brethren who are in bondage?
   _____
   _____
   _____

2. Why was Lamoni's father furious? Will our family always support our righteous desires and actions? Why or why not?

3. What do we learn about charity and mercy from this chapter?

* * * * *

Alma 21

Basic:

1. Who is involved?

2. What is being taught?

3. Why is this important?

4. How do I apply what is taught?

   _____
   _____

5. Will we always have success while on the Lord's errand? What do we learn from Aaron about trials?

   _____
   _____
   _____
   _____

Invitation:

Make a family mission plan, outlining goals you wish to accomplish in inviting others to come unto Christ. If you have a mission plan, review your progress and commit to it.

Bonus:

1. Why do you think Aaron did not have the success of Ammon? What does this mean to you?

   _____
   _____
   _____
   _____

2. Why would the Amalekites be unwilling to hear the gospel? Why are their hearts hardened?

   _____
   _____
   _____
   _____

3. Why is religious freedom important? How can we sponsor religious freedom, even in a Christian country?

   _____
   _____

_____

* * * * *

Alma 22

Basic:

1. Who is involved?

2. What is being taught?

3. Why is this important?

4. How do I apply what is taught?

5. How does Aaron teach Lamoni's father? Why would he employ this teaching method?

Invitation:

Ask someone about their beliefs in God.

Bonus:

1. What doctrines did Aaron teach Lamoni's father? Why would this matter to his eventual conversion?

   _____
   _____
   _____
   _____

2. Why was the Lamanite King converted? How does this relate to us, as members of the church?

   _____
   _____
   _____
   _____

*   *   *   *   *

Alma 23

Basic:

1. Who is involved?

   _____

2. What is being taught?

   _____
   _____

3. Why is this important?

   _____
   _____

4. How do I apply what is taught?
   _____
   _____

5. What does religious freedom mean to you? Why would it be important enough to Mormon to include in his abridgment?
   _____
   _____
   _____
   _____

Invitation:

Perform some Family History, and learn more about those who share your name.

Bonus:

1. What does verse 6 mean to you?
   _____
   _____
   _____
   _____

2. Why did the Lamanites lay down their weapons of rebellion? How can we do the same?
   _____
   _____
   _____
   _____

3. Why would it be important for the Lamanites to become industrious? Why is this attribute valued by the church?
   _____
   _____
   _____
   _____

Alma 24

Basic:

1. Who is involved?
   _____

2. What is being taught?
   _____
   _____

3. Why is this important?
   _____
   _____

4. How do I apply what is taught?
   _____
   _____

5. Why are the Anti-Nephi-Lehies visited by angels? Why is their faith so powerful?
   _____
   _____
   _____
   _____

Invitation:

Memorize a scripture about faith.

Bonus:

1. Why are genealogies so important to the children of Lehi? Why do they associate themselves based on their lineage (Nephites being descendants of Nephi, Lamanites being descendants of Laman)?
   _____
   _____
   _____

2. Why did the Anti-Nephi-Lehies choose to die rather than wield weapons of war? Do we take our covenants this seriously? Why or why not?

3. Why did the Lord allow innocent people to die in this chapter? Why do bad things happen to good people?

*   *   *   *   *

Alma 25

Basic:

1. Who is involved?

2. What is being taught?

3. Why is this important?

4. How do I apply what is taught?

   _____
   _____

5. Why are the Lamanites converted? How were they prepared to join the covenant people?

   _____
   _____
   _____
   _____

Invitation:

Share your conversion story with a family member or friend.

Bonus:

1. Why are we taught about the conversion of Lamanites in these chapters? How does this apply to us and our conversion?

   _____
   _____
   _____
   _____

2. Why did the seed of the priests of Noah perish? Why is God just?

   _____
   _____
   _____
   _____

* * * * *

Alma 26

Basic:

1. Who is involved?
   _____

2. What is being taught?
   _____
   _____

3. Why is this important?
   _____
   _____

4. How do I apply what is taught?
   _____
   _____

5. Why does he use men like Ammon to bring souls unto repentance?
   _____
   _____
   _____
   _____

Invitation:

Spend time glorifying the Lord today.

Bonus:

1. How does the Lord strengthen his servants? In what ways will we qualify for the blessings of knowledge?
   _____
   _____
   _____

2. How is the power of God connected to his comprehension of all things?

* * * * *

Alma 27

Basic:

1. Who is involved?

2. What is being taught?

3. Why is this important?

4. How do I apply what is taught?

5. Why were the people of Anti-Nephi-Lehi led to safety? How does the Lord lead us to safety?

_____
_____

Invitation:

    Take time to compliment a friend or acquaintance today.

Bonus:

1. How can we have friendships like Ammon and Alma? What made their joy so great?
_____
_____
_____
_____

2. How can we be welcoming of refugees of sin?
_____
_____
_____
_____

3. Why are titles so important in this chapter? These people are referred to as "Anti-Nephi-Lehies" and "The People of Ammon;" why would that matter to the Book of Mormon narrative?
_____
_____
_____
_____

    *   *   *   *   *

Alma 28

Basic:

1. Who is involved?
   _____

2. What is being taught?
   _____
   _____

3. Why is this important?
   _____
   _____

4. How do I apply what is taught?
   _____
   _____

5. What do we learn about wickedness and happiness in this chapter?
   _____
   _____
   _____
   _____

Invitation:

Make a happiness journal where you can write about your blessings and what brings you joy.

Bonus:

1. What does verse 6 teach us about the actions we should take when consumed by sorrow?
   _____
   _____
   _____

2. How would you describe the mood of this chapter? What feelings does the author convey?

___

* * * * *

Alma 29

Basic:

1. Who is involved?

2. What is being taught?

3. Why is this important?

4. How do I apply what is taught?

5. Why does Alma wish to teach repentance with angelic zeal? Do you?

_____
_____

Invitation:

    Make a list of your righteous desires. What duties do you wish you could do if granted angelic authority?

Bonus:

1. Why does the Lord call teachers and missionaries in each dispensation? Why is teaching important to the Lord?

_____
_____
_____
_____

2. When have you been proud of the work of someone else? Why is Alma happy about the success of Ammon and the other sons of Mosiah?

_____
_____
_____
_____

*   *   *   *   *

Alma 30

Basic:

1. Who is involved?

_____

2. What is being taught?

_____

3. Why is this important?

4. How do I apply what is taught?

5. What are some of the lies taught by Korihor? Are they still popular today?

Invitation:

   Share your testimony that God is our loving Heavenly Father.

Bonus:

1. How has your faith in Heavenly Father been built? What has taught you that there is a God?

2. How will Satan try and discredit our faith? Why does he use others to attack and belittle our beliefs?

3. What do we learn from Korihor's demise? Why is it important to avoid the honors and praise of men?

_____

* * * * *

Alma 31

Basic:

1. Who is involved?

2. What is being taught?

3. Why is this important?

4. How do I apply what is taught?

5. What do we learn from Alma's decision to preach to the Zoramites? Why was it important to him?

Invitation:

    Pray from your heart for those outside your faith.

Bonus:

1. What does this chapter teach about our role as disciples of Christ and the covenant people? How is our calling and election made sure?

2. What does this chapter teach about prayer? How can you avoid praying from a Rameumptom?

* * * * *

Alma 32

Basic:

1. Who is involved?

2. What is being taught?

3. Why is this important?

   _____
   _____

4. How do I apply what is taught?

   _____
   _____

5. Why did Alma teach the humble and the poor? What does this instance teach us about being effective with our talents and time?

   _____
   _____
   _____
   _____

Invitation:

Memorize a scripture about faith.

Bonus:

1. Why is the word of God compared to a seed? How do we let this seed grow in our hearts?

   _____
   _____
   _____
   _____

2. What is the connection between eternal life and the word of God? And how does faith make that connection?

   _____
   _____
   _____
   _____

Alma 33

Basic:

1. Who is involved?
   _____

2. What is being taught?
   _____
   _____

3. Why is this important?
   _____
   _____

4. How do I apply what is taught?
   _____
   _____

5. Why should we pray and worship in all places?
   _____
   _____
   _____
   _____

Invitation:

Offer a prayer or study your scriptures in a new setting or environment today.

Bonus:

1. What does the doctrine of mercy mean to you? How does this relate to grace?
   _____
   _____
   _____

2. Why did Alma use the brass serpent to teach about Christ? Why was this symbol used by Moses?

_____

* * * * *

Alma 34

Basic:

1. Who is involved?

2. What is being taught?

3. Why is this important?

4. How do I apply what is taught?

5. What does the Atonement mean to you? How does this chapter increase your understanding?

Invitation:

    Reflect on why the Atonement matters to you. Share your testimony of Jesus Christ with someone.

Bonus:

1. Why was the Atonement so necessary? How did it meet the demands of the Creation and the Fall?

2. What does this chapter teach about the Plan of Salvation? How are these principles tied together (salvation, atonement, sacrifice, redemption, faith & repentance, prayer, etc)?

*   *   *   *   *

Alma 35

Basic:

1. Who is involved?

2. What is being taught?

3. Why is this important?

   _____
   _____

4. How do I apply what is taught?

   _____
   _____

5. Why were the convert Zoramites kicked out of their city? What sacrifices have you made for your belief?

   _____
   _____
   _____
   _____

Invitation:

Reach out to someone in your congregation and help them feel loved.

Bonus:

1. Why is it that you can sorrow for the wickedness of others? Why would our Father in Heaven do this to us?

   _____
   _____
   _____

2. How can you be welcoming of recent converts? Why is friendship and fellowship important to conversion?

   _____
   _____
   _____
   _____

Alma 36

Basic:

1. Who is involved?

2. What is being taught?

3. Why is this important?

4. How do I apply what is taught?

5. Why would Alma share his conversion story with his son?

Invitation:

Share your conversion story with a friend or loved one today.

Bonus:

1. Why would Alma feel the pains of a damned soul? Was this necessary to his development of faith?

2. How can we have a fullness of joy after our conversion? What has brought you peace and happiness?

* * * * *

Alma 37

Basic:

1. Who is involved?

2. What is being taught?

3. Why is this important?

4. How do I apply what is taught?

5. Why are the scriptures preserved? What does this mean to you individually?

_____
_____

Invitation:

Make a list of things you've learned or blessings you've gained from scripture study.

Bonus:

1. Why should we avoid secret oaths and combinations? Why are these acts the work of Satan?

_____
_____
_____
_____

2. What does it mean to "counsel with the Lord"? How is more than saying prayers?

_____
_____
_____
_____

3. Why is it important to you to read about the destruction of the Nephites and the Jaredites?

_____
_____
_____
_____

*   *   *   *   *

Alma 38

Basic:

1. Who is involved?
   _____

2. What is being taught?
   _____
   _____

3. Why is this important?
   _____
   _____

4. How do I apply what is taught?
   _____
   _____

5. What advice does Alma have for Shiblon? Do you relate to this chapter, why or why not?
   _____
   _____
   _____
   _____

Invitation:

Research "light of Christ" in the Topical Guide.

Bonus:

1. What does it mean to bridle your passions? Why would we have these impulses and desires if we need to control them?
   _____
   _____
   _____

2. How is Christ the light and life of your world?

_____
_____
_____
_____

* * * * *

Alma 39

Basic:

1. Who is involved?
   _____

2. What is being taught?
   _____
   _____

3. Why is this important?
   _____
   _____

4. How do I apply what is taught?
   _____
   _____

5. How has living the law of Chastity blessed your life? Why are there sorrows attached to sexual transgression?
   _____
   _____

_____
_____

Invitation:

    Watch/read/listen to the talk by Elder Bednar titled "We Believe in Being Chaste."

Bonus:

1. How is the Atonement of Christ applicable to all? Why is he the Savior of the whole earth?

_____
_____
_____
_____

2. How does the story of Corianton connect to Matthew 5:14-16? How will our example impact our missionary efforts?

_____
_____
_____
_____

*   *   *   *   *

Alma 40

Basic:

1. Who is involved?

_____

2. What is being taught?

_____

3. Why is this important?

4. How do I apply what is taught?

5. What does this chapter teach about the Resurrection?

Invitation:

Memorize a scripture about resurrection.

Bonus:

1. Why would Alma teach his son Corianton about the Plan of Happiness? Why is this doctrine important to you?

2. Compare and contrast verses 12 and 14. Why would Mormon include these descriptions?

Alma 41

Basic:

1. Who is involved?

2. What is being taught?

3. Why is this important?

4. How do I apply what is taught?

5. Why is wickedness never happiness? Why is this phrase so popular in talks, lessons, and discussions?

Invitation:

Discuss with a friend or family member how obedience has impacted your happiness.

Bonus:

1. Why would the restoration of our characteristics be an important part of the resurrection?

2. Is the description of paradise or spirit prison more motivational to you? Why are we granted endless happiness or endless misery?

* * * * *

Alma 42

Basic:

1. Who is involved?

2. What is being taught?

3. Why is this important?

4. How do I apply what is taught?

5. Why is mortality a gift? Why is it a time to repent and serve God?

_____
_____

Invitation:

    Map out the Plan of Salvation, using specific verses from this chapter.

Bonus:

1. How does this chapter teach the doctrines of mercy and justice? How does Alma connect these two?

_____
_____
_____
_____

2. What does this chapter teach you about redemption and repentance? Why is penitence important to your salvation?

_____
_____
_____
_____

3. Reflect on the doctrines from Alma 39-42. How are these chapters connected? What is an overarching theme?

_____
_____
_____
_____

*   *   *   *   *

Alma 43

Basic:

1. Who is involved?

2. What is being taught?

3. Why is this important?

4. How do I apply what is taught?

5. Why would Alma and his sons be engaged together in missionary work? When have you worked with your family in inviting souls unto Christ?

Invitation:

Watch the video, "Unto All the World: Travels of the Apostles" on LDS.org about missionary work in Brazil.

Bonus:

1. Why do the dissenters become Lamanites? Why are haters so consumed with attacking and belittling?

2. How can we defend our rights, our religion, and our families from the antichrists of our day?

_____

*   *   *   *   *

Alma 44

Basic:

1. Who is involved?

2. What is being taught?

3. Why is this important?

4. How do I apply what is taught?

5. What do we learn about the character of Captain Moroni in this chapter? How can we emulate his example?

_____
_____
_____

Invitation:

    Make a list of your heroes and heroines from the scriptures. Then outline what made them so great and memorable.

Bonus:

1. Why would Moroni seek to avoid conflict? Why was his offer so severe?

_____
_____
_____
_____

2. What did Moroni do when Zerahemnah rejected his offer?

_____
_____
_____
_____

*   *   *   *   *

Alma 45

Basic:

1. Who is involved?

_____

2. What is being taught?

_____

3. Why is this important?

4. How do I apply what is taught?

5. Why would Helaman bless and curse the land? How does this connect to his role as a spiritual leader?

Invitation:

Read the account from Church History about the impact of dissension, "Take Special Care of Your Family," on LDS.org.

Bonus:

1. Why was Alma taken up by the spirit? And why don't we know his fate?

2. Where does the dissension in the church come from? How can we prevent a similar fate in our congregations?

Alma 46

Basic:

1. Who is involved?
   _____

2. What is being taught?
   _____
   _____

3. Why is this important?
   _____
   _____

4. How do I apply what is taught?
   _____
   _____

5. How can aspiring lead to conspiring? What is the difference between the two?
   _____
   _____
   _____
   _____

Invitation:

Ponder on other defenders of civil rights and freedoms, including your favorites.

Bonus:

1. What does this chapter teach about politics? Patriotism? Religion?
   _____
   _____
   _____
   _____

2. Martin Luther King said, "Injustice anywhere is a threat to justice everywhere." What are your thoughts on Captain Moroni's relentless defense of freedom?

_____
_____
_____
_____

*   *   *   *   *

Alma 47

Basic:

1. Who is involved?
   _____

2. What is being taught?
   _____
   _____

3. Why is this important?
   _____
   _____

4. How do I apply what is taught?
   _____
   _____

5. What do we learn about Amalickiah's nature from this chapter? Why can he be considered an antichrist?
   _____
   _____

Invitation:

> Watch/read/listen to the talk by Sister Dalton, "A Return to Virtue."

Bonus:

1. What does this chapter teach about the consuming power of wickedness? How do we avoid the fate of the dissenters?

2. Why would the Lamanite general refuse to come down from his mountain? Why should we maintain our religious high ground?

3. What corrupted Amalickiah to engage in such gross wickedness? Why did he use treachery, murder, and intrigue to become the Lamanite king?

*   *   *   *   *

Alma 48

Basic:

1. Who is involved?
   _____

2. What is being taught?
   _____
   _____

3. Why is this important?
   _____
   _____

4. How do I apply what is taught?
   _____
   _____

5. What do we learn about fear mongers in this chapter? Warmongers?
   _____
   _____
   _____
   _____

Invitation:

Research scriptures on Fear in the Topical Guide and Index.

Bonus:

1. How does Moroni prepare for the impending war from Amalickiah? How can we relate this to our own lives?
   _____
   _____
   _____
   _____

2. How does this chapter relate to the Plan of Salvation? The doctrine of faith?
___
___
___
___

* * * * *

Alma 49

Basic:

1. Who is involved?
___

2. What is being taught?
___
___

3. Why is this important?
___
___

4. How do I apply what is taught?
___
___

5. Why was Amalickiah's oath to drink Moroni's blood a sin? Where and how did this obsession grow?
___
___
___

Invitation:

> Memorize a scripture on faith or testimony.

Bonus:

1. How is this story a metaphor for obedience? Temptation?
   _____
   _____
   _____
   _____

2. How can you fortify your faith against the Lamanite armies? Why was it important to defend the weakest cities?
   _____
   _____
   _____
   _____

* * * * *

Alma 50

Basic:

1. Who is involved?
   _____

2. What is being taught?
   _____
   _____

3. Why is this important?
   _____

4. How do I apply what is taught?

5. How does this chapter outline each step in Moroni's fortification process? Why is this necessary for us in our day?

Invitation:

> Forgive a grudge or mend a relationship today. Rebuild a bridge that has been burned in your life.

Bonus:

1. How does verse 20 relate to this chapter? Why would it be a good summary of the war chapters of Alma?

2. How can we figuratively build new cities in our lives? What can you do in your prosperity to grow and develop your spirituality?

* * * * *

Alma 51

Basic:

1. Who is involved?
   _____

2. What is being taught?
   _____
   _____

3. Why is this important?
   _____
   _____

4. How do I apply what is taught?
   _____
   _____

5. Why were the king-men a threat to Nephite society?
   _____
   _____
   _____
   _____

Invitation:

Outline the story of Teancum, his successes and how he aided the Nephite army.

Bonus:

1. What can we learn from Teancum in this chapter? What were his motivations for his actions?
   _____
   _____
   _____
   _____

2. Why did Moroni give an ultimatum to the king-men? Why was his punishment so severe?

    *   *   *   *   *

Alma 52

Basic:

1. Who is involved?

2. What is being taught?

3. Why is this important?

4. How do I apply what is taught?

5. Did the murder of Amalickiah end the war? Why or why not?

Invitation:

    Share your testimony of repentance and forgiveness with a family member or friend.

Bonus:

1. What do we learn about the forces of evil from this chapter? How can we prepare for people like Ammoron?

   _____
   _____
   _____
   _____

2. Why are Teancum and Lehi victorious? What does that mean to you personally?

   _____
   _____
   _____
   _____

*　*　*　*　*

Alma 53

Basic:

1. Who is involved?

   _____

2. What is being taught?

   _____
   _____

3. Why is this important?

   _____

4. How do I apply what is taught?

5. Why are the Lamanites prisoners put to work? What does this teach about the importance of work?

Invitation:

Review some paintings of the stripling warriors and reflect on their story.

Bonus:

1. Why are dissentions so detrimental to the Nephites? How can you apply this to business, education, politics, or your congregation?

2. Why did the stripling warriors choose Helaman as their leader? Who do you support as your leader?

* * * * *

Alma 54

Basic:

1. Who is involved?
   _____

2. What is being taught?
   _____
   _____

3. Why is this important?
   _____
   _____

4. How do I apply what is taught?
   _____
   _____

5. What do we learn from this exchange by Moroni and Ammoron?
   _____
   _____
   _____
   _____

Invitation:

Perform an act of kindness today, maybe even redeem someone from bondage.

Bonus:

1. What is the justice of God mentioned in verse 6? And what is "the sword of His almighty wrath"?
   _____
   _____
   _____

2. What theological arguments does Ammoron make with Moroni? How are these arguments made today?

* * * * *

Alma 55

Basic:

1. Who is involved?

2. What is being taught?

3. Why is this important?

4. How do I apply what is taught?

5. Why was it important for Moroni to ask to exchange prisoners? Is negotiation always the answer to our problems, why or why not?

Invitation:

    Ponder why Moroni didn't meet the demands of Ammoron.

Bonus:

1. Compare and contrast this story with the exodus stories of Limhi's people (Mosiah 22) and Alma's people (Mosiah 24), also from Lamanite bondage. How is it similar and different from the Israelite Exodus in the Old Testament?

2. How does the battle of Gid represent the spiritual battles we face today? Why is violence not always the answer?

* * * * *

Alma 56

Basic:

1. Who is involved?

2. What is being taught?

3. Why is this important?

4. How do I apply what is taught?

5. What do we learn about covenants in this chapter? How do you personally live up to the title of "covenant keeper"?

Invitation:

Write out the promises you've made to your Heavenly Father, and the blessings He has given you because of your obedience.

Bonus:

1. What spiritual provisions and reinforcements do we obtain daily? Why does this strike fear into the adversary?

2. What was the source of courage spoken of in verse 45? How can we have similar courage?

_____

_____

* * * * *

Alma 57

Basic:

1. Who is involved?
   _____

2. What is being taught?
   _____
   _____

3. Why is this important?
   _____
   _____

4. How do I apply what is taught?
   _____
   _____

5. The chapter heading refers to Helaman's army as "Ammonite striplings." Why are they worthy of this comparison? How did they live up to the example of Ammon?
   _____
   _____
   _____
   _____

Invitation:

Memorize a scripture on obedience.

Bonus:

1. Again, the armies obsess over the flow of provisions. Why would this be the determining factor of a battle? What is this symbolic of?

2. What does verse 21 teach about obedience? Why did Helaman include this in his epistle to Moroni?

* * * * *

Alma 58

Basic:

1. Who is involved?

2. What is being taught?

3. Why is this important?

4. How do I apply what is taught?

5. Why does the Lord offer divine aid in this chapter? Why are the Ammonites preserved?

Invitation:

    Watch the video on LDS.org about spiritual crocodiles, a metaphor used by Elder Boyd K. Packer.

Bonus:

1. What are spiritual decoys that can lure us out of our strongholds? What must we do to defend our souls?

2. How does this chapter teach about deliverance? Peace? Comfort in trials?

          *   *   *   *   *

Alma 59

Basic:

1. Who is involved?
   _____

2. What is being taught?
   _____
   _____

3. Why is this important?
   _____
   _____

4. How do I apply what is taught?
   _____
   _____

5. Why would Moroni share the epistle he received from Helaman with all his people? Why would this be a source of motivation?
   _____
   _____
   _____
   _____

Invitation:

Find a motivational quote or meme on LDS.org and set it as your phone background, or a desktop picture.

Bonus:

1. What does this chapter teach about setbacks? Why is our path to salvation not a straight line?
   _____
   _____

2. What does verse 12 teach about the effects of loss? Can we really blame the chief captains for their reaction?

* * * * *

Alma 60

Basic:

1. Who is involved?

2. What is being taught?

3. Why is this important?

4. How do I apply what is taught?

5. Why was Moroni angry with the government? What were his motivations for his epistle?

_____
_____
_____

Invitation:

    Get a full night's rest tonight, and feed your spirit by praying and studying the scriptures.

Bonus:

1. In what ways have you seen fatigue, apathy, and tiredness affect your life? How can we fight this weakness?

_____
_____
_____
_____

2. Why is indifference a sin? How come you can't stand on the sidelines and refuse to pick sides?

_____
_____
_____
_____

    *   *   *   *   *

Alma 61

Basic:

1. Who is involved?

_____

2. What is being taught?

   _____
   _____

3. Why is this important?

   _____
   _____

4. How do I apply what is taught?

   _____
   _____

5. How did Pahoran react to Moroni's epistle? Why did he choose to not be offended despite being justified?

   _____
   _____
   _____
   _____

Invitation:

   Ponder a time when you chose to not be offended by the words or actions of others.

Bonus:

1. Why are the king-men again the source of upheaval in the government? What does this teach us about political machinations?

   _____
   _____
   _____
   _____

2. What rebellions have you participated in? Have they been justified, or were you merely "kicking against the pricks" (D&C 121:38)?

   _____
   _____

_____
_____

* * * * *

Alma 62

Basic:

1. Who is involved?
   _____

2. What is being taught?
   _____
   _____

3. Why is this important?
   _____
   _____

4. How do I apply what is taught?
   _____
   _____

5. Why does Moroni mourn in verse 2? How are rebels and rebellions tools used by Satan in his war of wickedness?
   _____
   _____
   _____
   _____

Invitation:

   Show some mercy today.

Bonus:

1. Why is it that justice cannot be mocked? Why did the king-men receive trial and punishment "according to the law"?

_____
_____
_____
_____

2. Where do we see mercy in this chapter? Why is it connected to the themes of justice?

_____
_____
_____
_____

* * * * *

Alma 63

Basic:

1. Who is involved?

_____

2. What is being taught?

_____
_____

3. Why is this important?

_____
_____

4. How do I apply what is taught?

    _____
    _____

5. What is the end of Shiblon's narrative? Did he live up to the counsel and expectations of his father (Alma 38)?

    _____
    _____
    _____
    _____

Invitation:

Read over your patriarchal blessing and ponder the Lord's plan for your life.

Bonus:

1. Why is Hagoth's story preserved? What does it teach us about fulfilling God's plan for us?

    _____
    _____
    _____
    _____

2. How many things are "thus ended" in this chapter? What meaning can you draw from it?

    _____
    _____
    _____
    _____

* * * * *

Helaman 1

Basic:

1. Who is involved?
   _____

2. What is being taught?
   _____
   _____

3. Why is this important?
   _____
   _____

4. How do I apply what is taught?
   _____
   _____

5. What were the motivations of the three sons of Pahoran? What can we tell about their character from this chapter?
   _____
   _____
   _____
   _____

Invitation:

Ponder over some big decisions you are making or could make soon. Outline the consequences of these actions.

Bonus:

1. What does this chapter, specifically Coriantumr, teach about strategy and problem-solving? Why must we think through our desires before we act?
   _____
   _____

2. Why do we have heroes like Moronihah in the Book of Mormon? How can we emulate his example when we aren't engaged in the military defense of our people?

_____

* * * * *

Helaman 2

Basic:

1. Who is involved?

2. What is being taught?

3. Why is this important?

4. How do I apply what is taught?

5. Why would the story of Gadianton and Kishkumen be preserved? How are their examples important to us in our day?
   _____
   _____
   _____
   _____

Invitation:

   Memorize a scripture on righteousness.

Bonus:

1. Why do you think Gadianton and Kishkumen were consumed by such gross wickedness? What led them down this path of murder, treachery, and deceit?
   _____
   _____
   _____
   _____

2. Why is flattery such a destructive force? How can we protect ourselves from this wicked action that led many of the Nephites to join the band of Kishkumen?
   _____
   _____
   _____
   _____

* * * * *

Helaman 3

Basic:

1. Who is involved?
   _____

2. What is being taught?

   _____
   _____

3. Why is this important?

   _____
   _____

4. How do I apply what is taught?

   _____
   _____

5. Do you think Mormon noticed the lack of contention when abridging these plates? Why would he mention that after the war chapters and the introduction of the Gadianton robbers?

   _____
   _____
   _____
   _____

Invitation:

   Ponder the history of the early Saints and the beginnings of the restored Church.

Bonus:

1. Why would a large group of Nephites flee to the north countries? Why were they determined to settle in a land devoid of timber and natural building materials?

   _____
   _____
   _____
   _____

2. How do verses 24 and 25 explain the church's influence? How is this prosperity linked to the mercy of Christ?

   _____

3. What actions are you taking today to fortify your faith in Christ? How are you fleeing from sin and wickedness?

* * * * *

Helaman 4

Basic:

1. Who is involved?

2. What is being taught?

3. Why is this important?

4. How do I apply what is taught?

5. Why would the Lamanites fear the Nephite dissenters? In the end, what do you think motivated the Lamanites to wage war against the Nephites?

_____
_____
_____
_____

Invitation:

Watch or listen to this talk by Elder M. Russell Ballard, "O That Cunning Plan of the Evil One," and reflect on the story he shares about addiction and obsession.

Bonus:

1. Why is verse 11 important to the Book of Mormon narrative? What does it imply about our actions, devotions, and obsessions today?

_____
_____
_____
_____

2. Why would Moronihah choose not to try and regain the cities and lands lost to the Lamanites? Why is it important to pick your battles?

_____
_____
_____
_____

*   *   *   *   *

Helaman 5

Basic:

1. Who is involved?
   _____

2. What is being taught?
   _____
   _____

3. Why is this important?
   _____
   _____

4. How do I apply what is taught?
   _____
   _____

5. What power is there in our names? How can we find motivation to be like the prophets in the Book of Mormon?
   _____
   _____
   _____
   _____

Invitation:

Watch the Mormon Message about missionary work, "Missionary Work: A Priesthood Duty," on LDS.org.

Bonus:

1. What does verse 9 mean to you? How does this strengthen your testimony of our Savior and his Atonement? How does it relate to verse 12?
   _____
   _____

2. How can we preach with power like Nephi and Lehi? Where did they draw their spiritual strength from and why did it make them great missionaries?

* * * * *

Helaman 6

Basic:

1. Who is involved?

2. What is being taught?

3. Why is this important?

4. How do I apply what is taught?

5. Why would the Lamanites become more righteous than the Nephites? And why is it so hard to believe that people can change and shed their wickedness?

_____
_____

Invitation:

    Take additional time to repent today.

Bonus:

1. What is the significance of the detailed description of the prosperity among the Nephites? Does this foreshadow the murders and treachery committed by the Gadianton robbers?

_____
_____
_____
_____

2. What historical figures does Helaman include when describing the influence of Satan? Why is his title "the author of all sin" and how does that impact you personally?

_____
_____
_____
_____

*   *   *   *   *

Helaman 7

Basic:

1. Who is involved?

_____

2. What is being taught?

_____

3. Why is this important?

4. How do I apply what is taught?

5. Have you ever felt the agony of soul described in verse 6? Why would Nephi be filled with such anguish and lament the actions of others?

Invitation:

Kneel down and offer a personal prayer out loud.

Bonus:

1. What do we learn about prayer and supplication from Nephi in this chapter? How is prayer a missionary tool even when we don't have towers in public squares?

2. If Nephi were to address you personally, what admonition would he give? What would he ask you to repent of?

Helaman 8

Basic:

1. Who is involved?
   _____

2. What is being taught?
   _____
   _____

3. Why is this important?
   _____
   _____

4. How do I apply what is taught?
   _____
   _____

5. Why is it that every prophet testified of Christ? Why would that be integral to their role as prophet, seer, and revelator?
   _____
   _____
   _____
   _____

Invitation:

Testify of Christ to a family member or friend.

Bonus:

1. Why was this the reaction of the people when they heard Nephi's lamentation? Why would the government officials take such offense to Nephi's prayer?
   _____
   _____

2. What was Nephi's reaction to their desire to kill him? How did he maintain his resolution in such dire circumstances?

* * * * *

Helaman 9

Basic:

1. Who is involved?

2. What is being taught?

3. Why is this important?

4. How do I apply what is taught?

5. What does it mean to fear God? Why did the five men who checked the judgment seat fall to the earth twice out of fear?

253

_____
_____
_____

Invitation:

    Write in your journal about a time you received revelation from the Spirit.

Bonus:

1. When have you been wrongly accused of something terrible? How does Nephi react to the accusations and threats of the people?
_____
_____
_____
_____

2. Why is this story so powerful? And how does it relate to the doctrines of faith and trials?
_____
_____
_____
_____

*   *   *   *   *

Helaman 10

Basic:

1. Who is involved?
_____

2. What is being taught?
_____

3. Why is this important?

4. How do I apply what is taught?

5. What praise does the Lord give Nephi in this chapter? How did Nephi qualify for the blessings given him by the Lord?

Invitation:

Ponder on the sealing power of temple covenants. Commit today to receive these blessings if you haven't already.

Bonus:

1. What does verse 5 teach about what we should pray about? Why is pray an alignment of our will to His, instead of a request form for blessings?

2. What effect do the miracles wrought by Nephi have on the people? Are signs really the answer to our doubts and our lack of faith, why or why not?

_____
_____

* * * * *

Helaman 11

Basic:

1. Who is involved?

2. What is being taught?

3. Why is this important?

4. How do I apply what is taught?

5. Why would a famine have a greater impact on the people than a war? Would the same be true today, why or why not?

Invitation:

Watch the Daily Bread series of Mormon Messages on LDS.org.

Bonus:

1. Can you think of other famines in the scriptures? What were the causes of these famines and how did the people react?

   _____
   _____
   _____
   _____

2. What tools and motivations did the Gadianton robbers employ in recruiting more dissenters? Why must we avoid being tempted by these same emotions today?

   _____
   _____
   _____
   _____

*   *   *   *   *

Helaman 12

Basic:

1. Who is involved?

   _____

2. What is being taught?

   _____
   _____

3. Why is this important?

   _____
   _____

4. How do I apply what is taught?
   _____
   _____

5. Does this chapter reinforce your trust in your fellowmen, why or why not? Why are we as people and individuals quickly led to wickedness and sin?
   _____
   _____
   _____
   _____

Invitation:

Identify a weakness you have and take steps today to overcome it.

Bonus:

1. What emotions do you feel as you read this section of the Book of Mormon? How can this section inspire or motivate you?
   _____
   _____
   _____
   _____

2. Why do the scriptures remind us of our weakness and carnal natures? Why is the comparison to our infallible, omnipotent God included in this chapter?
   _____
   _____
   _____
   _____

*   *   *   *   *

Helaman 13

Basic:

1. Who is involved?
   _____

2. What is being taught?
   _____
   _____

3. Why is this important?
   _____
   _____

4. How do I apply what is taught?
   _____
   _____

5. Why is the example of Samuel the Lamanite a powerful one? What are his strengths and his attributes that you can emulate?
   _____
   _____
   _____
   _____

Invitation:

Ponder on why the love of money is the root of all evil.

Bonus:

1. Why would Samuel's cursing be detrimental to the Nephite society? Why did Paul call the love of money "the root of all evil," (1 Tim. 6:10)?
   _____
   _____
   _____

2. When have you rejected or ignored the counsel of the prophets? Why must we sustain our current leaders and follow their advice?

_____
_____
_____
_____

* * * * *

Helaman 14

Basic:

1. Who is involved?
_____

2. What is being taught?
_____
_____

3. Why is this important?
_____
_____

4. How do I apply what is taught?
_____
_____

5. What is the significance of the signs promised by Samuel? Why would he describe the events leading up to the birth of our Savior?
_____

Invitation:

    Read or sing Hymn 193: I Stand All Amazed

Bonus:

1. What does this sermon by Samuel teach about the redemptive power of Jesus Christ? How is this doctrine connected to his teaching about the resurrection?

2. Compare verse 31 to Alma 3:26-27 and 2 Nephi 9:39. How is agency, or the gift to choose for ourselves, connected to the Atonement of Jesus Christ? Why are both of these doctrines vital to the Plan of Salvation?

* * * * *

Helaman 15

Basic:

1. Who is involved?

2. What is being taught?

3. Why is this important?

4. How do I apply what is taught?

5. When have you been chastened by the Lord of one of His servants? Why does Samuel the Lamanite claim that the Lord chastens the Nephites because He loves them?

Invitation:

Watch the Mormon Message about chastening, The Will of God

Bonus:

1. How can we be converted like the Lamanites? What made their faith firm and immovable?

2. Why would this chapter teach about mercy and righteousness following the doctrine of redemption in chapter 14? How do these two chapters relate and build upon each other?

_____
_____

* * * * *

Helaman 16

Basic:

1. Who is involved?
   _____

2. What is being taught?
   _____
   _____

3. Why is this important?
   _____
   _____

4. How do I apply what is taught?
   _____
   _____

5. In terms of baptisms, did Samuel the Lamanite see the fruits of his work? Do you think he felt like a successful missionary after the attempt on his life? Why or why not?
   _____
   _____
   _____

Invitation:

> Review paintings of Samuel the Lamanite on the wall and reflect on your feelings about this Book of Mormon prophet.

Bonus:

1. What differentiated the group of people who tried to kill Samuel and those who were baptized by Nephi? And why would some of the people see angels, and others harden their hearts?

   _____
   _____
   _____
   _____

2. What lie does Satan feed the people about faith in Jesus Christ? Why is this deceit so appealing to atheists and agnostics?

   _____
   _____
   _____
   _____

*　*　*　*　*

3 Nephi 1

Basic:

1. Who is involved?
   _____

2. What is being taught?
   _____
   _____

3. Why is this important?
   _____
   _____

4. How do I apply what is taught?
   _____
   _____

5. What effect did the signs and wonders have on the Nephites? Why would the majority still seek to slay the believers?
   _____
   _____
   _____
   _____

Invitation:

Memorize a scripture on trials or persecution.

Bonus:

1. Why is this chapter memorable? How can you relate to Nephi and his struggles?
   _____
   _____
   _____

2. What does the new star that arises symbolize? Why would this be the sign of the birth of Christ?
___
___
___
___

*　　*　　*　　*　　*

3 Nephi 2

Basic:

1. Who is involved?
___

2. What is being taught?
___
___

3. Why is this important?
___
___

4. How do I apply what is taught?
___
___

5. Describe the three sinful natures of having a hard heart, blind mind, and disbelief of miracles. How are they different and how are they connected?
___

_____
_____
_____

Invitation:

    Draw a castle and write out a plan for defending your faith against the servants of Satan.

Bonus:

1. Why would the Nephites and Lamanites unite to defend themselves against the Gadianton robbers? What does this story teach about the evils of terrorism?

_____
_____
_____
_____

2. Why are some afflictions and disadvantages due to our actions and some due to the actions of others? Why are we constantly warned against iniquity?

_____
_____
_____
_____

*   *   *   *   *

3 Nephi 3

Basic:

1. Who is involved?

_____

2. What is being taught?

_____

3. Why is this important?

4. How do I apply what is taught?

5. Why would Giddianhi make such an ostentatious demand? How has power corrupted his logic and training?

Invitation:

Forgive someone who has wronged you. Shed some pain associated with a grudge.

Bonus:

1. Why was Giddianhi obsessed with avenging his perceived wrongs? Why is it a sin to choose to be offended?

2. What do we learn from this exchange between Lachoneus send Giddianhi? Why should we dissect their communication and learn from this story?

3 Nephi 4

Basic:

1. Who is involved?

2. What is being taught?

3. Why is this important?

4. How do I apply what is taught?

5. Why did the Gadianton robbers fail? What is this symbolic of?

Invitation:

Share your testimony of obedience with a family member or friend.

Bonus:

1. Why would Gidgiddoni command his men to pursue the robbers to the edge of the wilderness? Why should we avoid fighting our temptations on the enemy's turf?

2. Have you ever felt grateful like the Nephites when they defeated the leaders of the Gadianton robbers (verses 29-33)? What does the imagery mean to you?

* * * * *

3 Nephi 5

Basic:

1. Who is involved?

2. What is being taught?

3. Why is this important?

4. How do I apply what is taught?

5. What does verse 3 teach about the doctrine of repentance? What steps are necessary to truly repent?

_____
_____
_____

Invitation:

    Review Hymn 169, As We Now Take the Sacrament, and reflect on its message of repentance.

Bonus:

1. Why is Mormon abridging these records? What purpose is he hoping to accomplish by compiling the history of the Nephites?

_____
_____
_____
_____

2. Why are we constantly taught about the gathering of Israel? How does this message apply to Mormon and the descendants of Lehi?

_____
_____
_____
_____

*   *   *   *   *

3 Nephi 6

Basic:

1. Who is involved?

_____

2. What is being taught?
_____
_____

3. Why is this important?
_____
_____

4. How do I apply what is taught?
_____
_____

5. Why are pride and hubris a common threat to character? Why are pride and prosperity a weakness and sin that exposes the worst in humanity?
_____
_____
_____
_____

Invitation:

Memorize a scripture about pride.

Bonus:

1. Why would the church suffer under dissensions and divisions? Why does our faith suffer from rebellion?
_____
_____
_____
_____

2. How are the prophets received among the Nephites? Why is this a pattern in the scriptures? How can we avoid this wickedness?
_____
_____

_____
_____

* * * * *

3 Nephi 7

Basic:

1. Who is involved?
   _____

2. What is being taught?
   _____
   _____

3. Why is this important?
   _____
   _____

4. How do I apply what is taught?
   _____
   _____

5. Review verses 17-21. How is Nephi considered a type of Christ? What similarities do they share that teach about the mission and ministry of our Savior?
   _____
   _____
   _____
   _____

Invitation:

> Write down an experience where you witnessed a miracle or the hand of God in your life.

Bonus:

1. Why are the political machinations preserved for the narrative? What does it warn us about in our day?

   _____
   _____
   _____
   _____

2. What miracles occur in Nephi's life during this chapter? What can we learn about being "in the world but not of the world" from his example?

   _____
   _____
   _____
   _____

* * * * *

3 Nephi 8

Basic:

1. Who is involved?

   _____

2. What is being taught?

   _____
   _____

3. Why is this important?

4. How do I apply what is taught?

5. How does this destruction relate to sin and wickedness? Will the consequences of our actions yield such dramatic results, why or why not?

Invitation:

Pray for those affected by calamities and disasters. Find ways to serve those who are desperately in need.

Bonus:

1. Why would darkness cover the land? Why is this the sign for the crucifixion of our Savior?

2. How does this chapter teach the doctrines of justice and mercy? How does this chapter teach about the Atonement?

3 Nephi 9

Basic:

1. Who is involved?
   _____

2. What is being taught?
   _____
   _____

3. Why is this important?
   _____
   _____

4. How do I apply what is taught?
   _____
   _____

5. How does this chapter teach about repentance? Obedience? Salvation?
   _____
   _____
   _____
   _____

Invitation:

Review Hymn 115, Come Ye Disconsolate, and reflect on its message of forgiveness.

Bonus:

1. What do we learn about the divinity and mission of Christ from this chapter? How are his roles defined and explained through imagery and metaphor?
   _____
   _____
   _____
   _____

2. How is the doctrine of Christ taught in this chapter? What do we learn about the process of faith, repentance, baptism, and enduring to the end?

_____

* * * * *

3 Nephi 10

Basic:

1. Who is involved?

_____

2. What is being taught?

_____
_____

3. Why is this important?

_____
_____

4. How do I apply what is taught?

_____
_____

5. Why is the image of the hen so powerful? And what do the differences in these repetitions (verses 4, 5, & 6) teach about the Savior's love?

_____
_____

Invitation:

Testify of the Savior's love to someone new today.

Bonus:

1. Why were the prophets slain for testifying of Christ? Why were they asked to preach repentance if the people were going to kill them?

2. What does the silence represent to you? Why was their silence for many hours instead of more moaning, wailing, and cries of anguish?

* * * * *

3 Nephi 11

Basic:

1. Who is involved?

2. What is being taught?

3. Why is this important?

   _____
   _____

4. How do I apply what is taught?

   _____
   _____

5. Why would Heavenly Father testify of his Beloved Son? What other instances in the scriptures contain this declaration?

   _____
   _____
   _____
   _____

Invitation:

Ponder over the relationship of the Godhead: God the Father, God the Son, and the Holy Ghost.

Bonus:

1. What message does the Savior bring in his appearance to the remaining Nephites and Lamanites? How is this message different than his post-resurrection appearance to his apostles in the Old World?

   _____
   _____
   _____
   _____

2. Why would the Savior invite each individual to touch his wounds and feel the prints? Why is the Atonement a personal relationship?

   _____
   _____
   _____

3. How does this chapter impact your relationship with Christ? How does it fortify your testimony of Him?

* * * * *

3 Nephi 12

Basic:

1. Who is involved?

2. What is being taught?

3. Why is this important?

4. How do I apply what is taught?

5. Why was the first order of business calling the twelve disciples? Why is Christ so quick to establish His church and restore the priesthood?

_____
_____
_____

Invitation:

    Make a minor goal that will lead you toward perfection Christ.

Bonus:

1. Why is this chapter often called the Sermon at the Temple? Why would it be similar to his teachings in Jerusalem?

_____
_____
_____
_____

2. What do we learn about the law of Moses from this chapter? Why does Christ fulfill the law?

_____
_____
_____
_____

* * * * *

3 Nephi 13

Basic:

1. Who is involved?

_____

2. What is being taught?

_____

3. Why is this important?

4. How do I apply what is taught?

5. How does Christ teach about prayer? Why does he use imagery and example to teach this doctrine?

Invitation:

    Memorize a scripture about prayer.

Bonus:

1. What does it mean to "lay up treasures in heaven"? How do you personally invest in heavenly treasures?

2. Why does Christ admonish his disciples (and apostles in the New Testament) not to care about their worldly appearance? How can you apply this principle to your discipleship?

3 Nephi 14

Basic:

1. Who is involved?
   _____

2. What is being taught?
   _____
   _____

3. Why is this important?
   _____
   _____

4. How do I apply what is taught?
   _____
   _____

5. Why would our Savior, Redeemer, and Mediator command us not to judge? With these roles, why would he condemn unrighteous judgments?
   _____
   _____
   _____
   _____

Invitation:

Avoid judging others, gossiping, and treating others unfairly today.

Bonus:

1. Why are false prophets a scourge to the church? How can false prophets affect your personal testimony and conversion?
   _____
   _____
   _____

2. Why does Christ teach us to do the will of the Father? How has the Son of God magnified and exemplified this attitude of humility?

* * * * *

3 Nephi 15

Basic:

1. Who is involved?

2. What is being taught?

3. Why is this important?

4. How do I apply what is taught?

5. Why would the Nephites struggle with the fulfillment of the law of Moses? How do you struggle with old things passing away?

_____
_____
_____
_____

Invitation:

> Give something up that is holding you back, bringing you down, or keeping you away from Christ.

Bonus:

1. Why is the metaphor of Christ as the good shepherd so powerful? Why does it matter to the Jews, the Nephites, and to you?

   _____
   _____
   _____
   _____

2. How have you felt like a lost sheep? How have you felt like the shepherd leaving the ninety-nine?

   _____
   _____
   _____
   _____

*   *   *   *   *

3 Nephi 16

Basic:

1. Who is involved?

   _____

2. What is being taught?

   _____
   _____

3. Why is this important?

   _____
   _____

4. How do I apply what is taught?

   _____
   _____

5. Why does Christ tell the Nephites that he has other sheep, not in the Americas nor in Jerusalem, that he must visit? How does this admission elaborate his role as Savior for the whole earth?

   _____
   _____
   _____
   _____

Invitation:

   Ponder over Christ's title of the Good Shepard.

Bonus:

1. Why would the gospel go to the Gentiles first and then the house of Israel? How have you seen this prophecy fulfilled?

   _____
   _____
   _____

2. Why does Christ teach about the gathering of Israel and latter-day missionary efforts? How did those truths resonate with the Nephites? How do they resonate with you?

   _____
   _____

_____

_____

* * * * *

3 Nephi 17

Basic:

1. Who is involved?

2. What is being taught?

3. Why is this important?

4. How do I apply what is taught?

5. Why would Christ ask us to ponder and pray for understanding? Why is this a principle and pattern of heaven?

Invitation:

Sing the song, Search, Ponder, and Pray in the Children's Songbook.

Bonus:

1. Christ repeatedly made it known that he had to leave. But what made him stay? And what happened because he stayed?

2. What does this chapter teach about charity and service? How can we give priority to the things that matter most?

* * * * *

3 Nephi 18

Basic:

1. Who is involved?

2. What is being taught?

3. Why is this important?

4. How do I apply what is taught?

   _____
   _____

5. What does verse 12 mean to you? Why would partaking of the sacrament mean you are building upon the rock of Christ?

   _____
   _____
   _____
   _____

Invitation:

   Do something today to build your faith upon the rock of Christ.

Bonus:

1. What commandments does Christ give in this chapter? How do they relate to and build upon each other?

   _____
   _____
   _____
   _____

2. What does this chapter teach about repentance? Why is there a discussion on those who do not repent?

   _____
   _____
   _____
   _____

* * * * *

3 Nephi 19

Basic:

1. Who is involved?
   _____

2. What is being taught?
   _____
   _____

3. Why is this important?
   _____
   _____

4. How do I apply what is taught?
   _____
   _____

5. How did the people react when Christ left them? Why is this important to know, and how can we emulate it today?
   _____
   _____
   _____
   _____

Invitation:

Take time to minister to someone today.

Bonus:

1. How did the twelve disciples minister to the people? How is this different than administering?
   _____
   _____
   _____

2. What pattern does Christ follow when he appears to the people? Why is this important?

3. Why were the prayers of Christ so important and meaningful?

* * * * *

3 Nephi 20

Basic:

1. Who is involved?

2. What is being taught?

3. Why is this important?

4. How do I apply what is taught?

5. Why would Christ administer the sacrament to the descendants of Lehi again, merely a day later?

Invitation:

Ponder over your baptismal covenants and the sacramental prayers.

Bonus:

1. Why would the descendants of Jacob inherit the Americas? What does this show about the promises made to the covenant people?

2. What similarities does Moses have with our Savior? What other prophets are types of Christ?

* * * * *

3 Nephi 21

Basic:

1. Who is involved?
   _____

2. What is being taught?
   _____
   _____

3. Why is this important?
   _____
   _____

4. How do I apply what is taught?
   _____
   _____

5. What is the connection between the Book of Mormon and the gathering of Israel? How are their purposes met in the last dispensation?
   _____
   _____
   _____
   _____

Invitation:

Write your testimony of the Book of Mormon in the blank pages at the beginning of your copy.

Bonus:

1. Why is the pattern of obedience stressed once again? Why is it a law of heaven that if we obey we prosper, and if we disobey we are destroyed?
   _____
   _____

2. Why will Israel build the New Jerusalem? Why is this another name for Zion?

* * * * *

3 Nephi 22

Basic:

1. Who is involved?

2. What is being taught?

3. Why is this important?

4. How do I apply what is taught?

5. Why would the Savior quote this passage from Isaiah? Why did it resonate with the Nephites and the people of Isaiah's day?

_____
_____
_____

Invitation:

    Show mercy or tenderness to someone today.

Bonus:

1. Why are stakes the metaphor used by Isaiah and the Lord? How is this a symbol for the units of the church?

_____
_____
_____
_____

2. What imagery does Isaiah use to teach about the gathering of Israel? Why are these images and symbols meaningful to you?

_____
_____
_____
_____

*   *   *   *   *

3 Nephi 23

Basic:

1. Who is involved?

_____

2. What is being taught?

_____

3. Why is this important?

4. How do I apply what is taught?

5. Why does the Savior command us to search the scriptures and learn from the prophets? Why is this an important step towards discipleship?

Invitation:

Share you testimony of the scriptures with someone new today.

Bonus:

1. What does this chapter teach about the importance of scripture? What is Christ's attitude towards the records kept by the ancient prophets?

2. Why are the words of Samuel the Lamanite added to the records? Why would his prophecies matter to our Savior and to us?

3 Nephi 24

Basic:

1. Who is involved?
   _____

2. What is being taught?
   _____
   _____

3. Why is this important?
   _____
   _____

4. How do I apply what is taught?
   _____
   _____

5. Why does Christ quote the prophet Malachi? Who else quotes Malachi in the scriptures?
   _____
   _____
   _____
   _____

Invitation:

Read through your book of remembrance. Cherish and treasure your journal(s).

Bonus:

1. What does this revelation reveal about the Restoration? How does it apply to the latter-day church?
   _____
   _____
   _____

2. What commandments are repeated in this chapter? Why are they worth repeating to the Nephites? To us?

_____
_____
_____
_____

*   *   *   *   *

3 Nephi 25

Basic:

1. Who is involved?
   _____

2. What is being taught?
   _____
   _____

3. Why is this important?
   _____
   _____

4. How do I apply what is taught?
   _____
   _____

5. What does verse 1 mean to you? Why does this precede the other prophecies contained in this chapter?
   _____
   _____

Invitation:

    If possible, visit the temple. If not, view pictures of the temple.

Bonus:

1. What is the mission and ministry of Elijah? Why was he given the keys relevant to the Restoration and the gathering of Israel?

2. How have you felt the spirit of Elijah? What can you do to better serve the Lord by redeeming the dead?

*   *   *   *   *

3 Nephi 26

Basic:

1. Who is involved?

2. What is being taught?

3. Why is this important?

4. How do I apply what is taught?

5. Why would Christ expound unto the multitude? How is this important to conversion?

Invitation:

Map out the events of the Creation. Ponder on its importance.

Bonus:

1. Why should we learn all things, from the beginning to the end of time? Why is the history of the Earth and its people important to discipleship?

2. How have you witnessed babes and children uttering marvelous truths? Why are children more in tune with the spirit and divine truth than adults?

3 Nephi 27

Basic:

1. Who is involved?

2. What is being taught?

3. Why is this important?

4. How do I apply what is taught?

5. What do we learn about the power of unity in verse 1? How can we emulate this experience in our families, our relationships, and our wards?

Invitation:

Review paintings of the Savior and ponder on your testimony of Him.

Bonus:

1. What does this chapter teach about prayer and the answers we will receive? When Christ appears, what does he tell the disciples?

2. How does the Holy Ghost sanctify us? What does that mean to you personally?

_____

* * * * *

3 Nephi 28

Basic:

1. Who is involved?

2. What is being taught?

3. Why is this important?

4. How do I apply what is taught?

5. Why was the desire of the nine disciples good? Why was the secret desire of the three even greater? How can we emulate this love and desire in our lives?

Invitation:

    Reflect on Hymn 125, How Gentle God's Commands.

Bonus:

1. How do we cultivate righteous desires in our heart? How can we devote ourselves to serving Christ and his children?

2. Why do we have so much description about the powers and lives of the three Nephites? How does this chapter build or increase your faith?

* * * * *

3 Nephi 29

Basic:

1. Who is involved?

2. What is being taught?

3. Why is this important?
   _____
   _____

4. How do I apply what is taught?
   _____
   _____

5. What is the purpose of the Book of Mormon? How does it accomplish its intentions?
   _____
   _____
   _____
   _____

Invitation:

Talk to someone about the Book of Mormon, its history, its purpose, or the blessings from studying it.

Bonus:

1. Why is the Lord devoted to the gathering of Israel? How can we emulate this devotion in our covenants, promises, and oaths?
   _____
   _____
   _____

2. Why is the latter-day dispensation an important principle of the gospel? Why is it repeatedly discussed in the scriptures?
   _____
   _____
   _____

3 Nephi 30

Basic:

1. Who is involved?
   _____

2. What is being taught?
   _____
   _____

3. Why is this important?
   _____
   _____

4. How do I apply what is taught?
   _____
   _____

5. In what ways are you considered a Gentile? And how are you considered a member of the House of Israel?
   _____
   _____
   _____
   _____

Invitation:

Memorize a scripture about repentance.

Bonus:

1. Why is this commandment from Christ applicable to all? Why does it matter to you?
   _____
   _____
   _____

2. Why is this chapter a perfect ending to the book of 3 Nephi? How does it prepare you for the events of 4 Nephi?

_____
_____
_____
_____

* * * * *

4 Nephi

Basic:

1. Who is involved?
   _____

2. What is being taught?
   _____
   _____

3. Why is this important?
   _____
   _____

4. How do I apply what is taught?
   _____
   _____

5. How does this chapter reflect the millennial reign of Christ? How can our study of the Nephites prepare us for the end of days?
   _____
   _____
   _____
   _____

Invitation:

Talk to your family about the importance of faith in Jesus Christ. Look for a way to nurture the faith of someone else today.

Bonus:

1. How can we build Zion in our own lives? What directions does this chapter give about living as a community of Christ?
   _____
   _____

_____
_____

2. Why did the descendants of the people choose wickedness over the paradisiacal Zion that their parents built? Why would anyone rebel against such a harmonious society?

_____
_____
_____
_____

*   *   *   *   *

Mormon 1

Basic:

1. Who is involved?
   ___

2. What is being taught?
   ___
   ___

3. Why is this important?
   ___
   ___

4. How do I apply what is taught?
   ___
   ___

5. Why would the wickedness of the people drive them to war? How is this an antithesis of the previous chapter?
   ___
   ___
   ___
   ___

Invitation:

Teach something, small or large, by the spirit this week.

Bonus:

1. Why does Ammaron call Mormon to be the keeper of the records? What other examples from the scriptures do we have of young men being called of God?
   ___
   ___

2. What wickedness is consuming the Nephites in this chapter? How do we avoid these sins?

* * * * *

Mormon 2

Basic:

1. Who is involved?

2. What is being taught?

3. Why is this important?

4. How do I apply what is taught?

5. What picture does verse 8 paint of the environment of Mormon's day? Why would he describe the wickedness as "one complete revolution throughout all the face of the land"?

_____
_____
_____
_____

Invitation:

Take time today to repent of something that you're struggling with.

Bonus:

1. What does this chapter teach about suffering and sorrow? What is the difference between godly sorrow and the suffering of the damned?

_____
_____
_____
_____

2. Why does Mormon carry the grief and anguish of the wickedness of his people? Why would our ability to empathize with others be a godly trait?

_____
_____
_____
_____

* * * * *

Mormon 3

Basic:

1. Who is involved?
   _____

2. What is being taught?
   _____
   _____

3. Why is this important?
   _____
   _____

4. How do I apply what is taught?
   _____
   _____

5. Why would Mormon cry repentance unto the people? How does he balance his responsibilities as military leader, record keeper, and prophet?
   _____
   _____
   _____
   _____

Invitation:

   Invite someone to read the Book of Mormon.

Bonus:

1. Why is hubris a tragic flaw in Shakespeare and in the scriptures? Why would reveling in our their own strength be a sin for the Nephites?
   _____
   _____
   _____

2. How does the Book of Mormon invite all of the twelve tribes to believe in the gospel? Why would it accomplish this task better than the Bible?

_____

* * * * *

Mormon 4

Basic:

1. Who is involved?

2. What is being taught?

3. Why is this important?

4. How do I apply what is taught?

5. Why does Mormon discuss the war and carnage of his day? How does this provide a spiritual lesson, despite the usual effects of violence on our spirits?

_____
_____
_____

Invitation:

    Make a worthy sacrifice today and reflect on your feelings.

Bonus:

1. What would you consider the greatest sin described in this chapter and why?

_____
_____
_____
_____

2. What wickedness do you need to avoid in your personal life? How do you protect yourself from the great wickedness of the Nephites?

_____
_____
_____
_____

    *   *   *   *   *

Mormon 5

Basic:

1. Who is involved?

_____

2. What is being taught?

_____

3. Why is this important?

4. How do I apply what is taught?

5. Why was Mormon without hope? In what things can we hope and trust, and what things are hopeless?

Invitation:

Reflect on the blessings of missionary work, specifically, how your efforts have changed your life.

Bonus:

1. What imagery resonates with you in this chapter? What makes it so powerful?

2. Why will the Lord scatter those who refuse to repent? What other consequences of sin can you think of?

Mormon 6

Basic:

1. Who is involved?

2. What is being taught?

3. Why is this important?

4. How do I apply what is taught?

5. Why would the Nephites gather to the land of Cumorah? Where should we gather in times of trial and affliction?

Invitation:

Stand in a holy place today. Write about your experience.

Bonus:

1. What do we learn in verse 6? How can we treasure and preserve the sacred writings of our lives?

2. How does this chapter teach the Plan of Salvation? What principles does this chapter explain concerning the events to come?

* * * * *

Mormon 7

Basic:

1. Who is involved?

2. What is being taught?

3. Why is this important?

4. How do I apply what is taught?

5. What invitations does Mormon extend in this chapter? How do they build upon each other? How do they apply to you?

Invitation:

>Review Hymn 180, Father in Heaven, We Do Believe, and ponder on its message of salvation.

Bonus:

1. What does Mormon explain about the relationship between the Bible and the Book of Mormon? How do they support each other?

2. Why is it important to know our ancestry? Why do our patriarchal blessings declare our lineage?

3. What hope do you find knowing you are "a remnant of the seed of Jacob"? Why would Mormon use the word remnant?

* * * * *

Mormon 8

Basic:

1. Who is involved?
   _____

2. What is being taught?
   _____
   _____

3. Why is this important?
   _____
   _____

4. How do I apply what is taught?
   _____

5. What lessons do you gain from this chapter? What does the destruction of the last Nephites represent?
   _____
   _____
   _____
   _____

Invitation:

Memorize a scripture about obedience or the blessings of righteousness.

Bonus:

1. What characterization does this chapter give of Moroni? What emotions filled his heart as he wrote these last words?
   _____
   _____
   _____

2. How is the doctrine of judgment, justice, and wrath explored in this chapter? How was Moroni's perspective affected by the events of his day?

* * * * *

Mormon 9

Basic:

1. Who is involved?

2. What is being taught?

3. Why is this important?

4. How do I apply what is taught?

5. What invitations does Moroni extend in this chapter? Why does he write to those who don't believe in Christ?

Invitation:

    Make a list of spiritual gifts that you have, and a list of those gifts you want to develop.

Bonus:

1. How have miracles and signs not ceased? What are they dependent upon?

2. Why is wisdom a Christ-like attribute? Why would Moroni, who saw the destruction of his people, invite us to be wise in our judgments of these records?

                      *   *   *   *   *

Ether 1

Basic:

1. Who is involved?
   _____

2. What is being taught?
   _____
   _____

3. Why is this important?
   _____
   _____

4. How do I apply what is taught?
   _____
   _____

5. Why does Moroni include the records of the people of Jared? Why does he place them at the end of his abridgment?
   _____
   _____
   _____
   _____

Invitation:

Ponder over the hand of the Lord in your life, and His tender mercies.

Bonus:

1. What lessons do you gain from this story of the Tower of Babel? How does it expound upon the story in Genesis?
   _____
   _____

2. Why does the Lord promise to guide the family of Jared into a promised land? What does this journey represent?

* * * * *

Ether 2

Basic:

1. Who is involved?

2. What is being taught?

3. Why is this important?

4. How do I apply what is taught?

5. How can we prepare for our journey to the promised land? What could the promised land represent to you?

_____
_____
_____

Invitation:

    Make preparations for the future, such as saving money, or food storage, or educational endeavors.

Bonus:

1. Why is preparation a duty of discipleship? Why would the Lord encourage us to "prepare every needful thing" (D&C 88:119)?

_____
_____
_____
_____

2. How did the Lord respond to the Brother of Jared's questions? How direct is the Lord's counsel in your life?

_____
_____
_____
_____

* * * * *

Ether 3

Basic:

1. Who is involved?

_____

2. What is being taught?

   _____
   _____

3. Why is this important?

   _____
   _____

4. How do I apply what is taught?

   _____
   _____

5. What does the Brother of Jared say to the Lord? What does he include in his prayer, and why is this important?

   _____
   _____
   _____
   _____

Invitation:

   Do something to build or increase your faith today.

Bonus:

1. Why is this chapter a seminal lesson on faith? What preceded the miraculous appearance and what were the results?

   _____
   _____
   _____
   _____

2. How can you emulate the example of the Brother of Jared? What can you do to develop faith like him?

   _____
   _____

_____
_____

* * * * *

Ether 4

Basic:

1. Who is involved?
   _____

2. What is being taught?
   _____
   _____

3. Why is this important?
   _____
   _____

4. How do I apply what is taught?
   _____
   _____

5. What commandments does the Lord dictate in this chapter? How are they related to each other?
   _____
   _____
   _____
   _____

Invitation:

Take a leap of faith. Put your trust in the Lord and step outside of your comfort zone.

Bonus:

1. Why would the Lord seal the writings of the Brother of Jared until after He had been lifted up on the cross? Why would this story be saved until a later time?

2. What justification does the Lord give for keeping these things from the Nephites? Why would faith be necessary to receive these records?

* * * * *

Ether 5

Basic:

1. Who is involved?

2. What is being taught?

3. Why is this important?

4. How do I apply what is taught?
   _____
   _____

5. Why would Moroni insert this chapter into his abridgment of the record of the Jaredites? How does its placement benefit from the stories before and after it?
   _____
   _____
   _____
   _____

Invitation:

Ponder over the many witnesses and testimonies of the Book of Mormon.

Bonus:

1. What instruments will the Lord use to testify of the truthfulness of the Book of Mormon? Why would these testimonies be used, and not others?
   _____
   _____
   _____
   _____

2. What does verse 6 mean to you? Why would it matter if Moroni has authority or not?
   _____
   _____
   _____
   _____

*   *   *   *   *

Ether 6

Basic:

1. Who is involved?

2. What is being taught?

3. Why is this important?

4. How do I apply what is taught?

5. How does the Lord direct the barges to the promised land? How does He direct you in your trials?

Invitation:

Reflect on Hymn 131, More Holiness Give Me, and the goodness of the Lord.

Bonus:

1. How long were the Jaredites in their barges traveling to the promised land? What does this teach you about affliction and deliverance?

2. What do the people do when they land? How have you expressed your gratitude to the Lord?

3. Why was there a concern about appointing a king over the people? What were the arguments for and against a king?

* * * * *

Ether 7

Basic:

1. Who is involved?

2. What is being taught?

3. Why is this important?

4. How do I apply what is taught?
   _____
   _____

5. Who ruled in righteousness and who didn't? What lessons does Moroni want us to learn?
   _____
   _____
   _____
   _____

Invitation:

Ponder over your personal idols, and do something to distance yourself from worshiping them.

Bonus:

1. What is the role of the prophets in this chapter? Why would the lord wall them to achieve this purpose?
   _____
   _____
   _____
   _____

2. What sins are the people guilty of? And how are these sins manifested in our day?
   _____
   _____
   _____
   _____

*   *   *   *   *

Ether 8

Basic:

1. Who is involved?
   _____

2. What is being taught?
   _____
   _____

3. Why is this important?
   _____
   _____

4. How do I apply what is taught?
   _____
   _____

5. What were the consequences of the strife and contention in the kingdom? Why should we eliminate these cancers from our relationships?
   _____
   _____
   _____
   _____

Invitation:

Make a plan to avoid the evils of secret combinations.

Bonus:

1. What were the motivations for Akish and his band? What led them to become so wicked?
   _____
   _____
   _____

2. Why are secret combinations condemned by the Lord? Why are they machinations of the devil to ensnare our souls?

3. How is this warning applicable to you personally? Why would Moroni want to prevent secret combinations from destroying our freedoms today?

*   *   *   *   *

Ether 9

Basic:

1. Who is involved?

2. What is being taught?

3. Why is this important?

4. How do I apply what is taught?

_____
_____

5. How does the kingdom pass from one person to another? What does this reveal about corruption, power, and wealth?

_____
_____
_____
_____

Invitation:

Share your testimony of repentance and its blessings with someone today.

Bonus:

1. What does this chapter imply about familial relationships? Why are families the central unit of society?

_____
_____
_____
_____

2. How have the prophets cried repentance in every dispensation? What have they asked you to repent of?

_____
_____
_____
_____

*   *   *   *   *

Ether 10

Basic:

1. Who is involved?
   _____

2. What is being taught?
   _____
   _____

3. Why is this important?
   _____
   _____

4. How do I apply what is taught?
   _____
   _____

5. How does this chapter teach the doctrine of agency? How does it illuminate the blessings and consequences tied to the give we have to choose for ourselves?
   _____
   _____
   _____
   _____

Invitation:

Make a list of things you would do if you were king for a day.

Bonus:

1. Why is righteousness directly tied to prosperity and blessings? How are these different from wealth and affluence?
   _____
   _____

2. Why does Moroni include description of the materials of the people? Why would it matter to describe the metals, riches, cloth, and tools of the Jaredites?

* * * * *

Ether 11

Basic:

1. Who is involved?

2. What is being taught?

3. Why is this important?

4. How do I apply what is taught?

5. Why were the prophets rejected and what did they do? How have you been persecuted for your beliefs or righteous actions?

Invitation:

> Watch a talk from the most recent General Conference. Reflect on what the prophets are teaching now.

Bonus:

1. Why does the Lord threaten the people with utter destruction? Why is this the consequence for their wickedness?

2. Why are we taught again the consequences of abandoning the Lord? Why is this lesson repeated over and over again in the scriptures?

* * * * *

Ether 12

Basic:

1. Who is involved?

2. What is being taught?

   _____
   _____

3. Why is this important?

   _____
   _____

4. How do I apply what is taught?

   _____
   _____

5. What did Ether do to magnify his calling? Why is the record of the Jaredites named after him instead of the original author, the Brother of Jared?

   _____
   _____
   _____
   _____

Invitation:

   Offer a prayer in humility.

Bonus:

1. What weaknesses are described in this chapter? How is it a defense for the Book of Mormon?

   _____
   _____
   _____
   _____

2. What does Moroni include as commentary in this chapter? Why would he insert these verses into his conclusion of the book of Ether?

   _____
   _____
   _____

3. What does this chapter teach about faith, hope, charity, and love?

* * * * *

Ether 13

Basic:

1. Who is involved?

2. What is being taught?

3. Why is this important?

4. How do I apply what is taught?

5. What does this chapter teach about the New Jerusalem? Why does this doctrine resonate with Ether, and why does it resonate with you?

_____
_____

Invitation:

    Do something today to build Zion, such as serve, love, mourn, consecrate, or donate.

Bonus:

1. Why won't the people accept the preaching of Ether? Why are their hearts hardened to the prophets?

   _____
   _____
   _____

2. What are the consequences of war? Why is it a human propensity to kill each other mercilessly?

   _____
   _____
   _____
   _____

    *   *   *   *   *

Ether 14

Basic:

1. Who is involved?

   _____

2. What is being taught?

   _____

3. Why is this important?

4. How do I apply what is taught?

5. How did the people react to the curse placed upon the land? What things have you cleaved unto in your life?

Invitation:

Donate to a charitable cause this week, either with your money or your time.

Bonus:

1. What does this chapter reveal about Coriantumr? How would you describe his character and his personality traits?

2. Why are verses 21 and 22 included in Moroni's abridgment? Why would he write about the carnage, the violence, and the desolation?

Ether 15

Basic:

1. Who is involved?
   _____

2. What is being taught?
   _____
   _____

3. Why is this important?
   _____
   _____

4. How do I apply what is taught?
   _____
   _____

5. What wrought the change of heart in Coriantumr? What has inspired you to repent, follow Christ, and forsake wideness in your life?
   _____
   _____
   _____
   _____

Invitation:

Pray for a change of heart, and nurture your desire to follow Christ.

Bonus:

1. What drove Shiz to his obsession? Why was he beyond reason, compromise, and diplomacy?
   _____
   _____
   _____

2. What can you learn about Shiz from verse 31? What does this verse reveal about the consequences of wickedness?

3. What do the last words of Ether mean to you? Why might he feel this way? Why would he end his record with this verse?

*   *   *   *   *

Moroni 1

Basic:

1. Who is involved?
   _____

2. What is being taught?
   _____
   _____

3. Why is this important?
   _____
   _____

4. How do I apply what is taught?
   _____
   _____

5. Why do you think Moroni wanted to end his abridgement after the book of Ether? Why did the Lord want Moroni to continue writing?
   _____
   _____
   _____
   _____

Invitation:

Reflect over a time where your plan was different than the Lord's.

Bonus:

1. What are the results of hatred? Why must we avoid planting the seed of contempt in our heart?
   _____
   _____

2. Why do the servants of Satan actively try to destroy the church of God? Why will you be persecuted because of your faith in Christ?

_____

* * * * *

Moroni 2

Basic:

1. Who is involved?

2. What is being taught?

3. Why is this important?

4. How do I apply what is taught?

5. Why would the gift of the Holy Ghost matter to Moroni? How do you think the Comforter directed, guided, and blessed his life?

345

_____
_____
_____

Invitation:

    Listen to and for the promptings of the Holy Ghost.

Bonus:

1. Why is the Holy Ghost a gift given through the priesthood? Why would it be necessary for Christ to give his twelve disciples this power and authority?

_____
_____
_____
_____

2. What does verse 3 mean to you? Why might the multitude not hear this conversation?

_____
_____
_____
_____

    *   *   *   *   *

Moroni 3

Basic:

1. Who is involved?

_____

2. What is being taught?

_____

3. Why is this important?

4. How do I apply what is taught?

5. Why are the twelve disciples of Christ called the elders of the church? Why is this title still used today?

Invitation:

    Ponder the blessings you've received from the priesthood.

Bonus:

1. What does this chapter reveal about the influence and power of the priesthood? Why is it organized and structured like it is?

2. What are the duties and responsibilities of the priesthood as outlined in this chapter? Why are these duties given to the priesthood holders?

Moroni 4

Basic:

1. Who is involved?
   _____

2. What is being taught?
   _____
   _____

3. Why is this important?
   _____
   _____

4. How do I apply what is taught?
   _____
   _____

5. Why would Christ dictate the process of administering the emblems of his flesh and blood? Why are these commandments given to us and were given to the Nephites of old?
   _____
   _____
   _____
   _____

Invitation:

Prepare yourself for the next time that you will partake of the Sacrament.

Bonus:

1. What doctrine is contained in the blessing on the bread? How does this prayer turn your heart to the Savior?
   _____
   _____

2. How does this prayer remind you of the blessings of your baptismal covenants? How does it remind you of all the covenants you have made?

* * * * *

Moroni 5

Basic:

1. Who is involved?

2. What is being taught?

3. Why is this important?

4. How do I apply what is taught?

5. Why are the sacramental prayers included in the Book of Mormon? Why would Moroni feel obligated to include them in his final writings?

Invitation:

> Write down the blessings you've received from the Sacrament.

Bonus:

1. What doctrine is contained in the blessing on the water? How does this prayer give you hope and peace?

2. Why must the sacramental prayers be spoken word-for-word? Why must they—and other ordinances—be repeated until the wording is perfect?

* * * * *

Moroni 6

Basic:

1. Who is involved?

2. What is being taught?

3. Why is this important?

4. How do I apply what is taught?

5. What are the "fruit" spoken of in verse 1? What evidences do we show to prove our readiness for baptism?

Invitation:

Listen to the song, When I am Baptized, from the Children's Songbook. Ponder over its imagery and its message of cleanliness.

Bonus:

1. Why are repentance and baptism connected? How does one influence the other?

2. Why did the church meet? And why did they meet often, instead of sporadically?

3. Why must the Holy Ghost direct and guide our church meetings? How can we do our part to invite the Spirit into our meetings?

_____

* * * * *

Moroni 7

Basic:

1. Who is involved?

2. What is being taught?

3. Why is this important?

4. How do I apply what is taught?

5. Why does Moroni include this sermon by Mormon? What does it teach about the traits of faith, hope, and charity?

_____
_____

Invitation:

    Offer an additional prayer to know good from evil. Seek understanding for a current concern.

Bonus:

1. Why does Mormon use the analogies of a good gift and an evil gift when discussing the doctrines of faith, hope, and charity? How does this illustrate the intentions behind what we do?

_____
_____
_____
_____

2. Why does Mormon outline the effects of good and evil on our hearts? Why are these concepts vital to our discipleship and testimonies?

_____
_____
_____
_____

* * * * *

Moroni 8

Basic:

1. Who is involved?

_____

2. What is being taught?

   _____
   _____

3. Why is this important?

   _____
   _____

4. How do I apply what is taught?

   _____
   _____

5. What lies lead the people to believe that baptism is necessary for little children? Why is this belief contrary to the Plan of Salvation?

   _____
   _____
   _____
   _____

Invitation:

   Share the fourth Article of Faith with a family member or friend today.

Bonus:

1. How does the Atonement allow all children to be made alive again? Why is it impossible for little children to sin?

   _____
   _____
   _____
   _____

2. Why would a better grasp of sin and our natures change our understanding of the atonement of Christ? How is His grace more meaningful after reading this chapter?

   _____
   _____

_____

* * * * *

Moroni 9

Basic:

1. Who is involved?

2. What is being taught?

3. Why is this important?

4. How do I apply what is taught?

5. What led the Nephites and the Lamanites to engage in such horrific and terrible crimes? What emotions do you feel reading about the depravity of these civilizations?

Invitation:

Look for an opportunity to show kindness for someone today.

Bonus:

1. Why is torturing one another a sin? Why would the Lord condemn those who engage in it?

   _____
   _____
   _____
   _____

2. What blessings does Mormon leave on his son Moroni? Why would these be beneficial to Moroni's destiny?

   _____
   _____
   _____
   _____

*   *   *   *   *

Moroni 10

Basic:

1. Who is involved?

   _____

2. What is being taught?

   _____
   _____

3. Why is this important?

   _____
   _____

4. How do I apply what is taught?

    _____
    _____

5. When have you prayed to know the truth of the Book of Mormon? How has it blessed your life?

    _____
    _____
    _____
    _____

Invitation:

Kneel down in prayer and act upon Moroni's promise. Pray to know if the Book of Mormon is true.

Bonus:

1. Why would Moroni exhort us to ponder the mercy of Christ? Why is this important for us to receive an answer to our prayers?

    _____
    _____
    _____
    _____

2. How many times does Moroni exhort us in this chapter? Why would he make such pleas to us as the reader?

    _____
    _____
    _____
    _____

3. Why does he end with a description and list of spiritual gifts after encouraging us to pray to know the truth? Why will we receive answers to our prayers when we ask in faith?

    _____
    _____

Conclusion

In conclusion, I hope this workbook has assisted you in your scripture studies. It is a compilation of a lot of work and dedicated study. I know the power of the scriptures, and want everyone to find joy and revelation in the Book of Mormon.

When we cherish the word of God, we find answers to our prayers, divine inspiration, and comfort to our souls. Our spirits need the nourishment that comes from scripture study.

The blessings of obedience are incredible. We cannot fully comprehend the rewards of righteousness. As we build our faith, and study earnestly the word of God, we will find our hearts filled with the Spirit. Doing the "Seminary Answers" of daily prayer, scripture study, weekly Sacrament attendance, and regular temple attendance ensure we are armed with the sword of the Spirit. We wear the armor of God when we keep His commandments.

Be sure to check out the other books in this series, and please share these aids with your friends and family. Let us all build the Kingdom of God.

Acknowledgments

I would like to thank Allison. She is my muse, my love, and my life. She brightens everything around her, and I am blessed to be a part of her life. Thank you for believing in me and letting me work so hard on this, and many other side projects. You're my favorite editor. I am so grateful for your compliments and your hugs.